PRAISE FOR THE

MW00831004

I just put down my copy of the Amish Pr[...] simple yet beautiful story because Joy related it so well. I feel like I know this man, John Schrock as well as Joy herself through this well woven storybook. I love the power of story because it pulls you into a picture of who God is that you would never have seen without a person like John living a very unconventional life. I also like the lens (as Joy shares in the end) that we get to see through as she shares very vulnerably her process of being his daughter and her search for her own identity in the midst of this. She masterfully relates the psychology behind the story and is so honest in her approach to sharing it. I am blown away that the word that I was able to give her played such a role in defining this mans life to us. We all get to see something in his story that creates faith for what God wants to do in our own lives. As you read this, you will find a story of great hope and encouragement in these pages that will transform your lens and perspective.

—**Shawn Bolz**, Author of *Translating God, God Secrets* & *Keys to Heaven's Economy;* www.bolzministries.com

"Write the book!"

When I heard those words spoken by Shawn Bolz to Joy Zipper I was shaken to the core. She was challenged to write a book about the exploits and stories of her father, John Schrock. Never in my life have I heard a personal prophecy so accurate and empowering. A message about a man that was my spiritual father and lifelong business partner. Immediately I sent the audio file around the world to our partners of the La Red Business Network. Many who knew John were moved to tears.

As one of the founders of the Network, I have had the opportunity of traveling internationally with John Schrock ministering for more than 25 years. This book captures the heart and the call of a Prophet of God. A prophetic voice to the Marketplace, Government and Educational spheres of influence. An early forerunner of the 5-fold ministry and that outpouring of God's Holy Spirit in the Amish and Mennonite community. John was to become a true World Changer!

The effort that Joy has put in has been amazing. True to detail and scope. Interviewing, documenting and writing a book with a beautiful openness to the supernatural part of John's life. In many ways she met her father in a whole new light. This is an incredible gift.

As I read of John's early life…*it moved me.*

As I was reminded of the early entrepreneur years building our companies together…*it inspired me.*

As I read of the massive move of the kingdom of God reliving those years… *it energized me.*

I trust that this book will move, inspire and energize you.

—BERNIE TORRENCE, Co-Founder of La Red Business Network

Watching my daughter, Joy, take on the challenge of boldly walking out this prophetic word was an incredible thing to behold. The fruit from all that laboring is a worthy account of the life of her dad and so many of our close friends, family and co-laborers. My Husband, John, was always seeking out the absolute will of our Heavenly Father. He lived a blessed life which was always a reminder to us of God's abundant love for His children. I pray that as you read of the radical stories and miracles that happened in our small, conservative community (and in our lives) that you see and feel God's love and faithfulness during a time when we just whole-heartedly pursued Him. Aside from all of that, I also want you to hold tight to one of John's favorite sayings: "Even if there was no Heaven or hell, this is still the best way to live."

—MARIE SCHROCK

The
AMISH PROPHET

ISBN: 0692081577
ISBN-13: 978-0692081570

The
AMISH PROPHET

From a Plain and Simple Life...
to a World Changer

JOY E. ZIPPER

CONTENTS

DEDICATION

First and foremost, I dedicate this book to God. It was He who asked me to write it and it was He who took me on the greatest "treasure hunt" of my life. My heart is overflowing with love and gratitude to Him.

I also dedicate this book to my father and mother. It was their relentless pursuit of truth and their unwillingness to live with anything less — that truly represents what is at the heart of these stories.

John 8:32 KJV, *"And ye shall know the truth, and the truth shall make you free."*

ACKNOWLEDGMENTS

I would like to thank Bernie Torrence, Jerry Anderson, and Pastor Caleb Klinge for their help walking me through this journey. Each of you have been nothing short of Spiritual Fathers to me. God chose each of you to help me through different aspects of this journey. God chose well for me. I will forever be grateful to each of you for your time, generosity, acceptance, understanding, guidance and unconditional love.

To my family — my husband, Alan, my children, Nicole David, and Nicholas, and my nephew John Codye, whom God has placed in my care for the last eight years. You have all had a front row seat to this journey. You have all paid a price in one way or another. Portions of this journey could not have been easy to watch. Thank you for never losing faith in me, for never losing faith in the journey and for never losing faith that God would take us through the narrow way to a life flowing with milk and honey. May none of us ever forget! Only God!

To Karl and Cindy Widder — what would I ever do without the two of you? No words could ever do justice to thank you for everything you've done for me. You were my daily example of what Christianity looks like when a person gets it right. You believed in me even when I no longer believed in myself. You pulled me back up time and time again. God must truly love me to have put you both in my life.

To Myles Weiss — God used you to help walk me through the darkness of grief. And in time, He used you to shine light and speak truth into Alan. You and Katharine have been a huge blessing in our lives. Some plant seeds and some water the seeds — you and Katharine have done both. We love you!

To my cousin Mark — there are no words that could ever do justice to thank you for the impact that you have made on my life and the lives of my family. I have never met anyone that represents the love of God and loves others as well as you do. You are truly one of the biggest and best surprises God brought into our lives — a cousin that I did not even know existed. God had you tucked away for such a time as this. Glory to God!

To Catherine Klinge — the relentless warrior and Light Girl evangelist God brought into my life. I did everything I could to avoid you, and yet you never gave up. I gave you every excuse in the book as to why I could not attend your Bible study meetings. Finally saying, the only way that I could attend is if it were in my own home. You jumped all over that. You didn't just push me out of my comfort zone — you kicked me out of my comfort zone. Today you are hanging out with Jesus and I visualize you just chatting up a storm. He has the pleasure of your company, while those of us left here still feel your loss. Thank you for never giving up on me!

To Shawn Bolz — thank you for being brave and thank

you for being obedient. Had you been anything less, I would have missed out on this amazing journey with God.

To all of the people that I interviewed over the last two years, thank you, thank you, thank you for these amazing stories.

FOREWORD

Preacher's Kids (PK's) have a unique perspective on the ups and downs of ministry. They see their parents in a way that others rarely do. They are directly impacted by both the hurts and triumphs that mom and dad experience as they pour their lives out in service to the Lord and His people.

When I first met Joy, I didn't realize she was a preacher's kid, or in her case — a prophet's daughter. I simply knew her as the gal who would come to services with her family and weep in the Presence of the Lord as she worshipped. The Spirit of God was encountering her, and deep was calling to deep.

I have gotten to know Joy and her family well over the last several years, and I have had the privilege of walking alongside her through the writing journey. Now I understand the healing process that was beginning when the Lord first brought her to our church family.

I was in the room at Bethel Church's Prophetic Conference when Joy received a prophetic word with the encouragement to write this book. I can attest to the authenticity in these pages, the price of writing them and the healing that the Holy Spirit brought in Joy along the way. She writes, "My own story was being rewritten by God as I was writing this book." I witnessed this powerful process happen.

Over the years, I have learned something about prophets and prophetic people. Prophets do not just speak a message — they are the message. John Schrock certainly had an important message from the Lord, a message that remains relevant to this day. His life is a message as well. You will appreciate getting to know John Schrock in the pages of this book. As you do, let the message of his life speak to you.

Though John Schrock's story is thoroughly unique, there are parts of it with which you will be able to identify. He had a supernatural encounter with God that forever changed his life, yet he was misunderstood and rejected as a result. Some of you have been wounded through a negative church experience. Others of you have done some wounding. The way John responded speaks to all of us — he chose to serve God with all of his heart rather than to draw back.

Perhaps you are a leader, and perhaps you've even been directly influenced by John's life and ministry. When you read about his humanity and struggles in these pages, do not be discouraged. Rather, take heart. Be encouraged as you see how the Lord equipped him, taught him, and brought him through. Hear the word of the Lord to your life: You can overcome.

Perhaps you are a Preacher's Kid, or the child of parents that serve in a leadership capacity. Being a PK is both a privilege and a burden. You will appreciate Joy's authenticity and openness in that regard. Let the testimony of her healing process wash over you. Know that the healing that she experienced from the Lord Jesus while writing this book is available to you as well.

If you are Amish, know this: John Schrock may have been one of the first Amish prophets, but he is certainly not the last. God has not called you to only follow a way of life — He's called you to follow Jesus. Let the life of one of your own, John Schrock, remind you of your First Love and the great plans that He has for your life. Anything is possible!

If you are not Amish, you will enjoy learning about these beautiful people, and hearing the story of God taking someone from relative obscurity to touch the nations of the world. The Lord is forever Jesus Christ of Nazareth. He is the one that raises up people from unexpected places to change the course of history.

—CALEB KLINGE,
New Life Church, Novato, CA

INTRODUCTION

Is there a Joy from Berlin?" I will forever remember when
I first heard this prophetic word spoken over Joy Zipper
by Shawn Bolz. My spirit wanted to leap from my body
in excitement when I heard the recorded prophecy. It was
a very powerful reminder that God is on the move on the
earth today, that He is a God of generations and that He
continues to be faithful to bring a harvest from seed that is
sown. God is not waiting on the rapture to speak, move and
act in supernatural and personal ways. That the Holy Spirit
sought Joy out to give this word to her through Shawn speaks
volumes of His love for her and His trust that she was the
woman to follow through on this hard-fought, tearful and
healing journey.

One of the things that struck me first about this prophecy
was the description Shawn used of John Schrock talking Jesus'
ear off... it immediately reminded me of a photo that sits on
my desk that Joy had given me right after her father passed on
to eternity of John sitting on a park bench with Jesus talking
with Him. Just this part of the word alone combined with
that photo was a huge confirmation that God was saying
something important to Joy. It was a tremendous lift just to

hear this little detail — God's intimate way of saying, "I know, I care and I am in this."

Reading this book is a beautiful reminder of why John's relationship with the Lord constantly inspired me. He had total reverence for the Father while maintaining a deep and abiding friendship with God. He had absolute faith and belief in what God said He would do. The simplicity in which he saw God's kingdom was profound and challenging to every person who heard from him. Truly, Jesus was his best friend followed closely by his wonderful wife, Marie.

John was an ironic combination of complete confidence and humility. He spoke with a surety most of us never truly possess because he hung every one of his thoughts and words on God's word. He had "Godfidence" — the confidence that comes when you have an intimate relationship with the Father and have been given access to understanding His love, His wisdom and His Kingdom. John was convinced beyond knowing and his faith was both life-affirming and life-giving.

John's understanding of the Bible and the Kingdom of God would have been an amazing achievement by any person but so much more so from an 8th grade educated Amish boy. God revealed Kingdom secrets to John and John shared the ones he could with anyone who would listen. He made the Kingdom of God simple... simple to understand and simple to be a part of. He taught how the application of Gods universal laws made life work and he also shared how God designed for the Holy Spirit to speak, move and be an active part in our everyday lives. John helped me and many others to experience

God's wisdom and power as personal and accessible parts of His nature rather than something we can only hope or aspire to tap into at some point. He put no limitations on God and eagerly sought for the Holy Spirit to bring His word alive in him.

Over decades, I had a front row seat to what an Amish Prophet looked like. I traveled with John as he spoke into the nations and have witnessed many of the words God spoke to him come to pass. I was blessed to experience several of the stories in this book firsthand with John and can confirm that Joy certainly did her due diligence in assembling a factual and compelling story.

This is a book to feed your faith, re-envision your purpose and encourage you on your own journey. Really all the things my mentor and spiritual father, Johnny Schrock, did for me. While this book pays a lovely and inspiring tribute to Joy's father, it is primarily a testament of God's love and healing. It is an expression of His grace and goodness and a wake-up call to the "more" that He has for each of us. It is a celebration of the miracle-working and sovereign power of God and the fact that His voice resounds today for those who will seek and listen.

Since John Schrock went to be with Jesus, I have watched the momentum of his legacy continue to accelerate rather than decline. The generational transfer has been incredible. Today, there are millions of people in more than 100 nations worldwide who are learning and being changed by the simple yet profound way he wrote and taught on how to live based on the word of God. In the last couple of years, I have seen teams of people from 24 nations come to the GPS training center in Berlin, Ohio to get training on how to implement values in all facets of society and to receive an impartation from the Spirit of God to go back and bring transformation to their countries. It is amazing and it is only God. These simple and profound values attract people from around the world because they are the truths of God that make life work. The application of God's truth un-complicates your life, increases the quality of your relationships, brings internal peace and makes way for His Kingdom to come.

Thank you, Joy, for accepting this Kingdom assignment. I know John is proud of you. The journey you have been on and the work you have done is just exceptional. I anticipate many people will be encouraged, find healing and come to know their Creator in a different way through not only this book but also the testimony of your life.

—Jerry Anderson
International President La Red Business Network

PROLOGUE

"Joy from Berlin"
A Prophetic Word from God

Spoken by Shawn Bolz - Prophetic Conference
Bethel Church, Redding, California
February 25th, 2015

Shawn Bolz: Is there, I don't know, I don't get this, but a Joy from... Joy from Germany? Or Berlin? That's what I saw. Joy from Berlin. Does that make sense? Are you Joy?

Joy: I am.

Shawn Bolz: Are you from Berlin?

Joy: I am.

Shawn Bolz: But you're not German.

Joy: I'm from Berlin, Ohio.

Shawn Bolz: Oh, that's cool! Berlin, Ohio. I didn't know there was one. *(Everyone begins to laugh.)* Oh that's so funny. From

Ohio — Berlin, Ohio — where you know... guten tag! This is really special. You're living in San Francisco.

Joy: Yes.

Shawn Bolz: This is good.

Joy: Unbelievable.

Shawn Bolz: Um, I'm just looking down because I'm nervous. I'm trying to get the rest of this. I'm trying to get more. Um, November, wow, November 9th, 2010 — John. Is this your father and he went to be with Jesus. And uh.

Joy: He was a prophet.

Shawn Bolz: He *was* a prophet. John Shock? Or?

Joy: John Schrock.

Shawn Bolz: I'm seeing him right now in heaven but he's behind you in heaven, like Jesus and your dad are behind you and he's smiling and Jesus is saying, "Write the book."

Joy: *(Big gasp.)* Oh!

Shawn Bolz: It's about his life. He has crazy stories, crazy. He's just a funny, crazy man that has a story to be told. It's like a hodgepodge collection of just who he was and what he prophesied. And I feel like the Lord is saying it's a catalyst opportunity because your dad is literally praying over you and your husband who is also close to your dad, who really respected your dad. I can see this. God is about to do something for you and your family and your dad is praying in heaven, but there is a story to be told and you're going to be in a learning journey as you tell the story for how to tell greater and greater stories. You're going to steward something with Him that's going to cause stewardship over your life. I see your dad is in all his glory. He looks around 30 years old. He looks so healthy — he's really fit. He's really fit like he would have been at that age and I feel like he's like so happy with Jesus right now. Like I'm just seeing Jesus and him are like best buddies. Like they, they're just like... he talks Jesus's ear off. This is like a man who knew how to — he had a gift of gab and he's talking Jesus's ear off all the time. And it's Jesus's pleasure to have him there. It's so awesome. But your dad is talking to Him about you and your husband and about your family and about your time in San Francisco, which is a divine assignment. And there's some things that you have to do there and there's some things that you have to become and your dad's part of your intercessory team. So just know that you're surrounded and it's time to do, and your dad, I'm telling you I know that was so painful for you. But it's now a celebration day because your dad is still alive. He's alive in heaven right now. Bless you. *(Speaks to everyone)* Wow. Those are holy moments, right?"

(A video of this prophetic word can also be found by visiting YouTube and searching "Shawn Bolz Joy from Berlin".)

This prophetic word led to the writing of the book you hold in your hands. I did not wake up one morning with a burning desire to be an author. This book is the result of my obedience to the divine assignment to which God called me.

The following pages contain the life story of my father, John E. Schrock, as well as the journey God took me on as I was gathering the information for this book.

I've always believed that life as we know it can completely

change in a moment. February 25th, 2015. This was one of those moments.

The prophetic word spoken by Shawn Bolz was the third prophetic word that I had received from Bethel Church in Redding, California. I attended the Prophetic Conference that night to get answers for the first two prophetic words that I had received, not to get another word. My goodness, I can't go back to that church any time soon! I just did not see this coming.

I had grown up in a church where prophetic words were commonplace. This wasn't a new concept to me. But what was new was that I had become the recipient of them.

For nearly five years prior, it seemed that everywhere I went I had become a "prophecy magnet." I did not understand what was happening nor did I need to know. I was just having fun chasing after Jesus. I did not realize that He was, in fact, chasing me.

I received many prophetic words over that five-year time span, but for the purposes of this story, I am focusing on the two prior to the one from Shawn Bolz. The two prior words created the circumstances that led me to attend the Prophetic Conference that evening.

The first prophetic word I received from Bethel Church came in an email in October 2014, from a man that I had never met. The sender of this email introduced himself and shared that he was instrumental in helping to write the curriculum for Bethel's School of Supernatural Ministry. This prophetic word referenced my business. I read his email, with little to no understanding, thanked this gentleman and moved on. I had no idea how important this word would become.

The second prophetic word was given at Bethel's Heaven in Business conference in January of 2015, as my businesses were chosen to be prophesied over. I have twenty minutes of recorded prophecy from that event.

After returning from the Heaven in Business Conference my team and I were excited after receiving clear direction — complete with words of knowledge to build our faith. We knew we were to judge these words, but what we were unprepared for was the amount of warfare that we were about to encounter.

The morning of the Prophetic Conference, February 25th, 2015, every email that I received regarding my business went from bad to worse. This solid, 30-year-old business was under attack. Everything that could go wrong was going wrong. Our largest distributor misplaced pallets of our products and in turn informed the retailers that we went out of business. Our followers on our Facebook page were being attacked by a professor and his students, more than likely due to our Non-GMO stance. And the list goes on and on. It was as if the forces of evil had targeted us.

By this time, I was at a loss as to what to do and to how to get through this. I had no answers.

Completely frustrated, I slammed my laptop computer shut, told my husband, Alan, to get ready as we were going to Bethel. I believed God would have answers for us at that conference. To say that I was mad would have been an understatement.

I had purchased the tickets to the Prophetic Conference as soon as they were available. I knew that this particular conference normally sold out quickly. This year, I was not going to miss it.

Had I not purchased these tickets in advance of the Heaven in Business conference, I am confident that we would not have gone to the prophetic conference even if tickets were still available. We already had more than enough to handle. Looking back, I can easily see how God set things up.

We drove to Redding at record speed that day. It was silent in the car other than the praise and worship music we were playing. I was in no mood to talk to anyone other than God. I was in the battle of my life and I knew God held the answers, but for some reason He had suddenly become silent on the subject.

After checking into our hotel, we made our way to the main campus at Bethel Church. There we met our friend, Charlotte, and together we made our way to our seats. As the worship started that evening, my spirit was still heavy and I was struggling to be there.

I am a worshiper at heart. There is typically nothing that brings peace to my spirit like worshipping my Creator. But this time I did not want to join in.

I felt disillusioned and confused. How was it possible that God would allow this warfare to overtake us? If He would give us these words, why wouldn't He protect us? To me, it was that simple.

I almost couldn't handle being in that environment. Everyone else was worshiping and praising God and I stood there numb — almost like I wasn't even there.

After several songs, I heard the music change and the beginning of my favorite song and I started to cry out to God through worship in a way that I rarely have.

As I entered into worship, I finally said, "Who cares. Who cares about anything but You, Jesus. I give it all to you. It's yours and whatever happens, happens." I was in the moment, nowhere else, just worshiping my beautiful Father.

Suddenly my entire being was on fire. Ah, there it was that amazing peace that falls as you surrender it all.

That night a gentleman by the name of Shawn Bolz was the guest speaker. I had never heard of him. I had no idea of the prophetic gifting that God had placed on him.

I listened intently as he delivered the message. The fire on me remained and I knew that I was exactly where God wanted me to be.

Shawn spoke that night that God will never give you a prophetic word without giving you the resources and the ability to walk it out. I nudged my husband and said, "This is why we are here." God was going to give us the answers we sought.

At the end of the message, Shawn delivered a prophetic word to one or two other people in attendance. I was amazed as I listened. I had never seen anyone with a prophetic gift that included such precise and specific words of knowledge as his.

Then he said, "Is there a Joy from Germany here?" Well,

well, well, here we go again. I was excited because I believed
God was about to give me another word regarding my
businesses — the next key so to speak.

I was not going to stand until I knew for sure that he was
calling me out. I could have easily made a connection with
Germany, because I am actually of German/Amish descent
and I worked closely in a partnership of sorts with a company
in Germany.

But I was waiting this out just in case there actually was a
Joy from Germany in attendance. Then he said, "Or Berlin?
That's what I saw. Joy from Berlin. Does that make sense?"
Finally, I stood to my feet.

Shawn proceeded with first the words of knowledge
and said, "You are living in San Francisco". I respond,
"Unbelievable." How does a person go from Berlin, Ohio
(Amish country) to San Francisco? That amazed me. He had
my full attention by that point.

Then he said the words, "November the 9th" and my heart
sank. Are you kidding me? I could not believe that God would
do this to me. What in the world was God thinking? He had
just exposed the greatest pain in my life — the death of my
father — on a huge platform.

I loved my dad beyond anyone in my life. We were like oil
and water. If you put the two of us in a room together it was
anyone's guess as to which one of us would be left standing.

My dad and I were each other's greatest adversaries and
we were each other's greatest allies. Try figuring out that
relationship. I spent a lifetime attempting to do just that.

In many ways I played the role as my father's keeper. The best analogy I can give you is that he threw the party and I was the cleanup crew. I always watched out for him. I had no problem whatsoever of going up against him if I knew he was wrong, or to defend him if I knew he was being accused unfairly.

The dynamics at play in our relationship were incredibly complex. But no matter how complex the relationship might have been there was no shortage of love between us.

All of the other prophetic words that I had received up until this encounter with Shawn Bolz were pretty much private. Unless you were part of my inner circle I did not share freely regarding the journey that I was on with God. Shawn's prophetic word exposed me and I felt incredibly vulnerable.

Had this not been a prophetic conference I am quite confident that I would not have said, "He was a prophet." I still can't believe those words came out of my mouth so freely.

I had only discovered that my dad was a prophet at his death bed. A prophetic word had been called in and spoken over him as he took his last breath. I was still reeling from that revelation more than three years later.

Then Shawn went on, "Jesus says, 'write the book.'" I gasped again. My dad and I held a conversation two months prior to his death regarding the possibility of a book being written on his life.

My husband was a huge fan of John Schrock and was constantly after me to write a book on my dad's life. I was more than a little annoyed, as my entire life, everyone was always in awe of my dad. My husband had become one of them.

Not that I didn't love my dad or know that he walked with authority from God Himself. I totally understood why people were in awe of him. Or so I thought.

But he was my dad and I struggled for my own identity. For most of my life I had been introduced as John Schrock's daughter.

As my dad and I spoke that day in the kitchen regarding a book on his life, we were throwing out ideas of what that book might look like. When Shawn said, "He has crazy stories. He's a crazy, funny man," he could not have been more accurate. My dad used to joke about how he was going to write a book called *Humility and How I Obtained It* and when you opened the book it would be filled with pictures of him. Oh, how I would cringe when he told stories like that from the pulpit.

We never came to a conclusion regarding what a book on his life might look like. But it certainly was a highly entertaining conversation as you would expect from my dad.

From "write the book" on I pretty much shut down. I became too aware of the platform this word was being given on. I wanted to crawl under my chair. I knew it was airing on Bethel.TV and I knew this was going to expose me to everyone back home in Berlin. I also knew that it would expose me to everyone that knew my dad and all those involved in the ministry my dad had founded.

It was quite a coincidence or perhaps a divine appointment that Pastor Caleb Klinge was at that meeting. Caleb pastored over New Life Church in Novato, California, where my family had been attending. I had no idea he would be attending this conference. I had seen him walking on the other side of the sanctuary prior to the service.

After the service, Pastor Caleb immediately made his way to me. I am quite certain he knew I would need to talk to him.

He shared with me that Shawn had been to New Life Church several years prior. He went on to say that at that time Shawn prophesied over the church. Pastor Caleb informed me that everything that Shawn had prophesied had come to pass. Well, that was encouraging. But what I wanted to know was what Shawn had actually said after "write the book." Pastor Caleb explained the best he could with what he remembered.

That night my husband and I could not have slept for more than several hours. We were both completely undone.

My husband was born Jewish but out of his love for me he attended every church meeting that I attended over the past five years. Trust me, that was no easy feat. I dragged him all over the place.

My husband witnessed as I experienced things that he totally did not understand. Fortunately, he had become fascinated with the journey that God had been taking me on as Alan watched from the sidelines. By this time, he was no longer able to reason things away as coincidences.

He, too, was being wooed by Jesus. This prophetic word just completely rocked his world.

The next day I was able to listen to the prophetic word in its entirety. Once again, I was undone. Shawn delivered a big word. I was literally facing a divine assignment from God.

Over the next two days at the Prophetic Conference, we couldn't walk four steps without being stopped and asked about the prophetic word. Everyone was celebrating it. Judging by my reaction, everyone thought they knew what it meant to me as Shawn was giving the word. But they didn't. Nor did I have the will to tell them differently. It was too complicated to explain.

Over the next two-and-a-half years, as I interviewed people for this book on my dad, I went through an incredible period of healing from my past. My own story was being rewritten by God as I was writing this book.

As I mentioned, my businesses were under attack and I just did not understand why God was asking me to do this. Out of obedience I stepped up to the plate. But I had no clue, not even the slightest clue as to how writing this book would profoundly change me.

I went through life pretty much the epitome of what you think of when you hear the term *preacher's kid*. And as I've written "the book", I have gone through the fire. I have yielded everything that I am and everything that I have to God. He has brought me out the other side a completely and utterly changed person. For God to have chosen me to write this book has become truly the most humbling experience of my life.

I about drove myself crazy at times trying to figure out where God was leading me, what that should look like, and how the pieces fit together.

I no longer care about any of that. I only care that every single day I am doing exactly what He wants me to do. He will take care of the rest.

After compiling all of this information and writing the book on my dad's life, I have nothing but respect for him. Today, I consider it a huge compliment to be told "you are just like your dad." Introduce me as "John Schrock's daughter," or as "Joy from Berlin," or as a "radical follower and lover of Jesus", and I'll wear all of those titles with pride.

This was a very difficult book to write due to how big of a life that my father led. I've broken the story down into categories, as trying to share it as it happened simultaneously would just be impossible to write and even more impossible for anyone to follow. As you read, I think you'll understand why very quickly.

This is the life story of my dad, The Amish Prophet — John E. Schrock, born and raised Old Order Amish into a plain and simple life. He left this life on earth on November 9th, 2011, and entered the gates of heaven as a world changer for Jesus. I am certain that he heard the words, "Well done, My good and faithful servant."

Peace, Love & Blessings,

Joy

CHAPTER ONE

Amish Life: 1940–1960s

In order for you to fully understand John's story, it is necessary to give you a bit of an education of the Amish culture back in the 1940s, 50's & 60's. These are the decades that I reference in the chapter regarding John's Amish years.

The Amish at that time were not like the Amish of today. They were very much separate from the rest of the world back then. There was no tourism in the area. The Amish were virtually unknown throughout the rest of the country except in the counties in which they resided. Even in those counties, they remained very much secluded from the rest of society.

Being Amish is similar to being Jewish. Both are considered to be a race as well as a religion. Unlike most subcultures, the Amish are unique in their ability not only to survive, but in their ability to thrive without much input from the outside world.

In those days, Amish were primarily farmers. Their farms

stayed within the family for generations. The family farm was passed down to one of the children. This was a common occurrence when the parents were no longer physically able to handle the day-to-day operations of the farm. The child that inherited the farm then moved their family into the main house. The parents then moved into what is referred to as a "Daudy Haus" — translated as grandpa's house. The Daudy Haus is a separate house, located closely to the main house. This allows the parents to maintain privacy and close proximity to the children in the event a need arises. The parents would have been well-taken care of and looked after by all of their children, but were primarily in the care of the one that inherited the farm.

Because the Amish are primarily farmers and their farms stay in their families for generations. They are generational thinkers. They often take into consideration the consequences of what decisions that they make today will have on future generations. They are willing to pay the price and make sacrifices in their own lives for the benefit of their children and the generations to come.

They are diversified farmers, meaning that they do not just grow corn or raise only cattle. They believe strongly and practice strict crop rotation to keep their soil healthy and in good condition. Nearly everything they eat they have grown or raised.

In those days making a trip to town for staples such as coffee, toilet paper, and cleaning supplies, was a big deal. Getting the horse and buggy ready and taking a trip into town could easily become an all-day event. Rarely did they hire drivers to take them into town, which is a common occurrence today. This meant it was necessary to be as self-sufficient as possible. Canning vegetables, meats and fruits was a normal way of life — allowing them to put back provisions to get the family through until the following year's harvest.

Many traditions have not changed. To this day, the Amish live without automobiles with their chosen mode of transportation still being horse and buggy. They live without electricity, telephones, radios or anything that they consider worldly. Their goal is to be a completely self-sufficient community with as little influence from the outside world as possible.

The Amish are often referred to as the "plain clothes" people. Their clothes are plain and all hand sewn. Only solid dark colors are permitted. The women's dresses are all made from the same pattern, with strict rules regarding the appropriate length. Women are not permitted to cut their hair and are always required to have their hair pulled up and covered with what they call a covering or bonnet. No jewelry or makeup is permitted.

During the week the men will primarily be found in work pants normally made from a dark navy-blue denim that accompanies a plain button-down shirt. Most of the time they will wear suspenders as belts are not permitted. On their heads you'll find broad-rimmed hats.

Neither men's nor women's clothing can have zippers — only buttons and pins.

Church Sundays are very formal and both men and women are required to wear their Sunday's best.

There are several reasons that the Amish have strict rules regarding clothing. One of the reasons is to ensure that there is no visible way for people to differentiate the wealth of the individual. It helps to keep competition of status in check. It also helps to keep people from becoming prideful.

The Amish do believe in Jesus Christ as the Son of God. Despite this, they do not believe that a person can know that they are saved. They cling to specific scriptures in the Bible and they build most of their theology around those passages. Their refusal to be worldly or use modern day technology comes from the scripture found in Romans 12:2 KJV *"And be not conformed to this world: but be ye transformed by the renewing of your mind, that ye may prove what is that good, and acceptable, and perfect, will of God."* In addition to select scripture, the Amish religion is also steeped with tradition.

Because the men are born to be farmers and the women are destined to be wives, mothers and homemakers, their education does not exceed that of an 8th-grade level. They learn only the very basics in English, reading, math, etc.

The Amish are primarily of German and Swiss decent. They speak what is referred to as Pennsylvania Dutch. Pennsylvania Dutch is the Schwebish dialect of German.

Very little affection is shown by the Amish and that includes affection to their children. Children are required to help with the chores on the farm and around the house. A good work ethic is instilled in them starting at a very young age. In this environment, children quickly learn that their "works" so to speak are what their value as a person is based upon.

As the children enter their teenage years they enter a stage known amongst the community as "rumspringa." This is translated as "running around" and this period normally lasts until marriage and/or when they join the church. It is during this time that you'll find the boys driving cars, both boys and girls dressing like the English (or "modern" townspeople) and basically sowing their wild oats. This is not necessarily encouraged; however, it is widely known and a blind eye is turned towards it by the community. This is to ensure that they get this "rumspringa" out of their system prior to marriage and/or joining the Amish church. The day they join the Amish church means that they fully intend to follow the ways and doctrine of the Amish religion.

Very rarely does anyone leave the Amish church/community. The consequences of doing so are swift and extremely painful. Leaving the religion is referred to in the Amish community as "jumping the fence."

Children are taught from birth that the rest of the world is basically evil. They are taught that if they leave the Amish, they cause not only themselves to go to hell, but condemn their parents as well. The Amish do not mince words or leave any doubt whatsoever of what the consequences will be. In addition to this, a person is also fully made aware that any such move would cause them to lose their entire family and all of their friends. The person is shunned. Excommunicated.

You are dead and none of them are permitted to speak to you or have anything to do with you whatsoever. At that point a fence jumper faces life alone — no inheritance, no family, no friends — alone to face the big, bad and scary world that they have only the most basic skills developed to survive in.

Although the Amish have their own set of issues, as do all people groups, overall, they are a peaceful and quiet community.

CHAPTER TWO

Amish and Conservative Mennonite Days

John E. Schrock was born on November 15th, 1931. He was the seventh child of nine children to Eli and Barbara Schrock who resided in Sugarcreek, Ohio. John oftentimes would say he was the next to the youngest by one. The youngest were in fact twins.

John was born and raised Old Order Amish. His father held the position of Bishop within the Amish church. Many people that attended services when Eli spoke tell the same story — he was no ordinary Amish Bishop. His messages were very compelling and he delivered them with conviction and authority.

John referred to his parents as beautiful people. He often said that he could not have asked for better parents. His father was strict but fair. They instilled an incredible work ethic into John, as is tradition with all Amish. John never heard his parents say the words, "I love you," although he knew without question that he was very much loved.

John's childhood was primarily spent working on the farm — plowing fields, feeding the animals and milking the cows. Their days started early and they worked hard to keep the farm pristine and to ensure the animals were well taken care of.

John was an incredibly bright and inquisitive child. With not much to do on the farm other than work, he found ways to entertain and challenge himself.

Later in this book in the chapter called "Foundational Lessons — Overcoming Fear" you will, in fact, discover one of those ways. It will give you a greater understanding of how John's mind worked as well as very specific personality traits that stayed with him throughout his life.

When John was about eight years old, his mother returned home from a shopping trip in town with a big, beautiful Bible storybook. It had all of the stories of the real heroes of the Bible and the acts of God that were done through the prophets, leaders, and the kings.

It was this Bible storybook that changed John's view on whom God was. It also presented him with a world-view and it made him think differently. As he read this book over and over and over again, it wasn't long before he started to ask his parents questions. Questions that very much challenged their own teachings.

One of those questions John asked, "Why doesn't God do today what He did back in the Bible days?"

To John it appeared that every time that God had a problem that needed to be solved, He spoke to a man and called him to solve the problem. God Himself did not solve the problem — He always spoke and used someone like Samson, Moses or Abraham.

When cultures were deteriorating or Israel needed correction — God raised up the standard — but He always used a person to accomplish it, a person that God would raise up to bring life and truth and restoration to the situation.

John also questioned, "Why God does not do the miracles today, the signs and wonders that He did back in the Bible days?"

His father would tell John that he was just too inquisitive and he asked too many questions. Eli said, "We are Amish and we live this way and we take things as they come. We live on the farm, mind our own business, keep our own customs, and our own religious beliefs."

No matter what his parents would say, John believed that the God of the Bible stories was alive and well and at work in people's lives and in the situations of the world. As a small Amish child at eight years of age he now had a belief that started to expand his mind. He started to believe in something bigger than he had been taught.

Over the next three to four years, John continued to read those bible stories over and over again. By this time, John fully understood that what he was feeling and thinking about God needed to stay between him and God. He knew his questions did nothing but create conflict with his parents and he knew he would hear the same answers. John had learned to have a silent belief and his beliefs continued to get stronger and stronger.

At the age of 12, as John was walking into the barn, he felt an unusual and unfamiliar presence. He knew someone or something was in the barn because he sensed something was different. As he looked around, he started to become a bit afraid.

Suddenly about fifteen feet from where he was standing, he saw an angel descending from the ceiling. The angel was dressed in all white, had clear blue eyes and was approximately seven feet tall. John stood there for a while looking at this beautiful sight, mesmerized by the angel's exquisite blue eyes. He smiled at it and the angel smiled back at him. The angel felt almost human, but John inherently knew it was an angel as no one from his community would ever be dressed in all white.

After a few moments, fear started to take hold because he knew the teachings of his community. He knew people would think there was something wrong with him because "normal people" do not see angels. As soon as his thoughts turned to fear, the angel disappeared, but not without leaving a profound impact on John. John felt the presence of that angel for the rest of his life. He believed and knew from that day forward that he had been assigned an angel.

John lived his teenage years knowing that the angel was always with him. He was a pretty typical kid who did some bad things, but the angel's presence was always with him. At times, John would return home after having spent the night out on the town with his buddies drinking and acting like a teenager, but when he laid his head on his pillow at night he wept because he felt so bad that the angel had been privy to his actions. The presence of this beautiful, blue-eyed angel kept John from ever going too far into sin. It helped to keep him in check.

This encounter with the angel had become the high point of John's life to date. It helped him through the difficult days of believing differently about God than his family and the rest of his community. He continued to maintain a silent belief.

Another supernatural encounter happened early in John's teenage years. This time God spoke to him through a vision. In this vision, God told John four things that he would experience in his life:

1. He would be a preacher and travel the world giving his testimony.
2. He would be a businessman.
3. God was going to release the spirit of Elijah on the earth. John was to watch for a sign in the sky that it had been fulfilled.
4. This was of a personal nature that John never shared with anyone.

Now remember, John was Amish at this time and he had never been outside of the state in which he was raised. To think that he would travel the world and give his testimony would have had to have been a stretch for anyone. But with John's childlike faith and these supernatural experiences, he simply believed God.

One day, when John was still in school, the teacher asked the students what they wanted to be when they grew up. John raised his hand high and with pride. When called upon, John said with assurance, "I want to be a preacher and a businessman." The entire class laughed because in their minds those two things could never go together. But John was convinced that what God had told him was true, regardless of what his classmates or anyone else believed.

Throughout John's life he had developed a love of music, particularly gospel and country. During his rumspringa years, John and his brother Mony (Emmanuel) both learned how to play the guitar and sing. The two of them and several others that played musical instruments performed at many events for the young people in the Amish community. They played at many corn-husking parties and were often called upon to provide the musical entertainment at parties held in the evenings after weddings.

The one thing that could be said about the young people from the Amish community during their rumspringa years was that they truly knew how to throw a party. They were wild back then. Alcohol ran as freely as dancing did. The Amish young people knew that their time was limited for them to enjoy "English" life with no rules and they certainly made the most of it.

It was also during John's rumspringa years where it would be permitted for him to drive a car. John did just that — he bought a car. Upon returning to his home, he parked the car at the end of the lane on the main road by their house.

Although the Amish turned their backs on the antics of their children during their rumspringa years, the children inherently knew not to draw unwanted attention to what they were doing. Parking the car in his parent's driveway was crossing a line that John knew should not be crossed.

After about two days of John owning the car, he became completely consumed with guilt. For John's entire life, he had been taught that driving a car is a sin and he just could not live with the burden of shame. He finally decided the only way to relieve the guilt was to return the car. Upon returning it, John discovered that he would not be able to get his money back. The salesperson told John he might as well keep the car. John said, "No, thank you. I'd rather sleep at night."

It appeared that there was a compromise that John was able to negotiate with himself regarding driving and owning a vehicle.

John spent two years in the early 1950's in 1W Service as an orderly at a hospital in Akron, Ohio. 1W Service was established by law for conscientious objectors. In lieu of military service, conscientious objectors were required to perform civilian work contributing to the maintenance of the national health, safety, or interest. As the Amish are conscientious objectors going into battle was absolutely prohibited.

It was at this time that John purchased a Harley-Davidson motorcycle to provide transportation to and from the hospital. John loved that motorcycle, particularly the fact that it had a suicide shifter. I've heard stories that John was seen more than once riding his Harley with his guitar strapped to his back. That is not hard for me to imagine — not even slightly. He truly was unconventional in every way.

Later in life, when John was asked why he was OK with owning a motorcycle and not a car, John would reply, "Because it only has two wheels instead of four" followed by a hearty laugh.

In John's early 20's, he attended the wedding of a friend. It was the custom that the young people stay upstairs while the women were preparing the meal downstairs. As John was making his way up the stairs, he encountered the most beautiful girl he had ever seen walking down the stairs. As the girl looked at him she started to lose her balance and nearly tripped.

This girl's name was Marie Erb, and she was indeed a beauty. She had black hair and green eyes, a gentle countenance and grace rarely found amongst the Amish. John was completely smitten by this girl. He was five years her senior.

With her father's permission, it wasn't long before the two of them started to date and shortly afterward they were going steady. They were both completely and utterly in love with each other.

Then one day Marie's parents, Mike and Fannie Erb,

attended revival meetings at Pleasant View Conservative Mennonite church. Upon return home that night, they announced that the minister gave an invitation to be saved and they both responded to the invitation. When John heard this news, he insisted that a person could not know that they were, in fact, saved. After all, that had been what he had been taught his entire life and nowhere in that Bible storybook had he learned any different.

Soon after Mike and Fannie were saved, they left the Amish church and became members of Pleasant View Conservative Mennonite church. This eventually led to Marie's dad's unwillingness to allow the two of them to continue to date. Mike wanted better for his daughter — he wanted to ensure that she, too, would be spending eternity in heaven.

There are several differences between the Amish and the Conservative Mennonite beliefs, particularly back in the 1950s. One being that the Conservative Mennonites believed a person can know that they are saved and the Amish believe that a person cannot know they are saved. This is literally interpreted by the Conservative Mennonite community that the Amish were, in fact, not saved. No one would want that for their child, including Mike and Fannie.

The biggest differences between the two are in regard to liberties. Unlike the Amish, the Conservative Mennonites are permitted to own and drive cars, they have electricity and indoor plumbing.

The Conservative Mennonite congregants are primarily made up of people that left the Amish church. This made many feel superior to the Amish as in their opinion they had taken a step up.

John was completely heartbroken and longed for Marie. He could not stop thinking about her no matter how hard he tried. He had no way of talking to her and their paths in life never crossed after their break-up. The decision made by Marie's father felt very final.

Then one day, a year and a half after their break-up, to John's surprise, he received a letter from Marie asking him to meet with her. They did, in fact, meet on New Year's Eve 1954, ushering in 1955 — a year which would represent great changes for them both.

It was at this meeting that the two decided that they could no longer live without the other. Marie was now eighteen years old. This meant that she no longer legally needed her parents' permission to get married. They knew their marriage ceremony would create major conflict as their parents were now of different religious beliefs. They also knew that no matter which religion they chose to follow, one of the two families would be unhappy. Not wanting to be married with all of this inevitable drama, they devised a plan that night to elope.

On Feb. 21st, 1955, with the help of several friends they recruited — two to be witnesses and one as a driver — John and Marie made their way to Indianapolis, Indiana.

They chose this neighboring state because they could have blood tests in the morning and be married later that same day. By sunset, John and Marie were married. The ceremony took place in a courthouse and they were officially declared husband and wife by a Justice of the Peace.

Upon their return as newlyweds, it soon became evident that they had agreed prior to marriage to join the Amish church. Regardless of John's questions, he was deeply committed to his family and the Amish way of life. This was well received by John's family and Marie's family knew that there was no chance of changing it.

John felt loyal to his dad. He could not comprehend leaving the Amish as his father was a Bishop and he knew the pain that it would cause his family. Marie adjusted to Amish life quickly as her parents had only recently left the Amish church themselves. It was the lifestyle that Marie was the most accustomed to.

After John and Marie were married in 1955, John was working for the Belden Brick Company in Sugarcreek, Ohio, as a general laborer. His Conservative Mennonite co-workers relentlessly challenged him, saying that the Bible scriptures themselves do not support the Amish religion's teachings.

Once again, he was facing the same arguments that his now father-in-law had made several years earlier.

Finally, after just wanting to put an end to the harassment, John decided to read the Bible for himself. These people presented him with specific scriptures that supported their beliefs.

As he started to read and research the Bible, it wasn't long before he was once again facing another dilemma — the same one that he had faced several other times in his life. He discovered a new truth in God's word and now he once again had to decide how these new truths were going to affect his life.

This led to many conversations with his own father. He was again challenging the Amish belief system, but this time he was armed with Biblical scripture, no longer just Bible stories. John was once again told by his father, "This is how we believe. This is our tradition. You need to quit asking questions and just accept it."

John continued to struggle within himself because he could not reconcile living with anything less than the truth. He had come to believe in a God much bigger than religious traditions.

The final straw for John with the Amish church would involve new laws they were incorporating regarding power lawn mowers. The Amish church was implementing a new rule that it would no longer be acceptable for their congregants to use power lawn mowers to cut their grass.

John was tired of the never-ending list of things that they were not permitted to do. By this time, John had been reading and studying the Bible long enough to know that you aren't going to find that in the Bible. This was, in fact, just another tradition that they were adding to the list. That was the day that John knew that they would inevitably be leaving the Amish church. His line in the sand was now drawn.

In mid-1957, John and Marie were invited to attend revival meetings at Sharon Conservative Mennonite Church located outside of Sugarcreek, Ohio.

They left the meeting after the first evening unable to make a decision when the invitation for salvation was given. But the following evening was a different story. That night they both accepted the invitation given to be saved. John wept and wept and left there knowing for the first time in his life that he was, in fact, forgiven and saved. He discovered the truth and the truth had now set him free.

Everyone in the community immediately noticed the difference in John. John described the conversion as things were no longer just black and white to him. He found himself taking more things into consideration when making decisions.

He often said even his own animals knew he was different, particularly his horse and the cats. Salvation had transformed him into a much gentler and kinder version of his previous self and it was apparent to everyone he came into contact with. Word on the street was that Johnny Schrock had, in fact, gotten saved.

John and Marie left the Amish church soon after they were saved. The backlash from the Amish community was swift and harsh. Perhaps this retaliation grew even more extreme than normal since John's father was an Amish Bishop and basically was unable to control his own son or to get him to see the light so to speak. Although the Amish had no telephones or modern transportation, word in the community traveled quickly.

Soon, John found himself being shunned and in one day, one decision he had lost his entire family, including many of his lifelong friends from the Amish community. The saving grace was that he was being very much embraced by the

Conservative Mennonite community. This was a huge coup for them. The son of a very popular Amish Bishop had seen the light and they could not have been more proud of this accomplishment.

In 1958, John's zest and zeal for these newfound truths led him to become an ordained minister in the Conservative Mennonite Church. He became an assistant pastor at Sharon Church — the same church he and Marie had gotten saved in. This led to the partial fulfillment of the first of four things that God had told John would happen in the vision.

John studied the Bible relentlessly. As the word opened itself up to him, he was continually discovering new truths that led to more and more freedom.

It wasn't long before John found himself sharing these newfound truths in his sermons from the pulpit — sermons that he soon discovered the Conservative Mennonite Church would consider controversial and against their religious beliefs.

One of the more notorious events that created extreme controversy happened the following week after another Pastor from the church had preached an entire message about the radio. This pastor stated that listening to the radio was wrong and it was sinful.

The following Sunday, John preached that Conservative Mennonites often make fun of the Amish regarding how ignorant they are because they believe everything is wrong, everything is sinful. The Amish teach cars are wrong, electricity is wrong and on and on he listed the things that are forbidden by the Amish church.

He went on to say, but we do the same thing. We teach the radio is wrong, the TV is wrong and continued to list all of the things that are forbidden by the Conservative Mennonite church. He said, "We aren't any different than the Amish. The only real difference is that our list of things that are wrong is just different from theirs." I'm sure you can imagine how well this message was received by the church leadership.

He gave the example, "A radio is just like a car, neither good nor bad. It's what you do with the radio that makes it good or bad." He said, "to the pure, all things are pure," and "blessed is the man that condemneth not himself in that thing which he alloweth, and I alloweth the radio if used for good." John was indeed a seeker of truth, not tradition.

Immediately after the service John was confronted by the Bishop. He said, "You can't preach like that at our church." John replied "I just did."

In order to try to keep John content and away from the majority of the church people, the leadership decided to create a mission outreach in New Bedford, Ohio, and to put John in charge of this outreach. A small group of congregants from Sharon Conservative Mennonite church followed him.

The first thing John decided to do at this new outreach church was to put an altar front and center at the church. There was no altar at Sharon church. As John studied the Bible, he realized that everything revolved around the altar. Even the temple itself in the Bible was secondary to the altar.

At Sharon church, when an invitation was given for salvation, people would raise their hands. Then those people would be escorted to a separate room in the church for prayer. John believed that people should not be ashamed of dedicating their lives to God. When altar calls were given people made their way to the front.

It wasn't long before the people at the mission outreach church started to shout out and become very vocal as John was delivering his sermon. They would shout out "amen" and "hallelujah." This was just another thing that was forbidden by the church.

But the biggest "to do" occurred when John started to teach out of the book of Acts, Chapter 2. He was teaching on the gifts of the Holy Spirit. This was considered radical teaching.

When he was confronted by the church leadership, John explained that what he was teaching was word for word out of the Bible. The Bishop adamantly replied that it was absolutely not permitted. John looked at him, held out his Bible and said, "Please tear out the parts of the Bible that I am not permitted to teach on."

I was born right at this time, the last day of 1960, into all of this chaos. The evening that my parents brought me home from the hospital, the executive committee from Sharon Church came to our home and officially removed John from his position and from the church.

Later one of John's friends shared the story of what happened that Sunday morning at Sharon church after John had been excommunicated. The pastor announced, "We have silenced John Schrock." One man stood up and said, "I was with him last night, you may have thrown him out, but he ain't silenced."

The backlash from being excommunicated from this group was once again very swift and very severe. John had now left an even a greater trail of religious bloodshed along the way and now they were being rejected by two separate religious groups. The Amish, Conservative Mennonite and Mennonites easily represented 80% of the population in that community.

By this time John was becoming fearless. He was in relentless pursuit of truth. He sought truth above tradition, the active work of the Holy Spirit above Amish and Conservative Mennonite culture and tradition. He was a radical from the starting gate and this was no time to stop. This newfound freedom would take him places that he never could have foreseen.

CHAPTER THREE

The Birth of the
Little White Church

Now John had been excommunicated from not one, but two religious groups. He realized that the chances of him fitting in with any churches in the area were slim-to-none. He was tired of the fight with religious-minded people.

All he wanted was to know the truth, to be free and to receive everything that Jesus had to offer. He was relentless in this pursuit and he did not care what anyone had to say. Those experiences at the hands of religious people did nothing but fuel him.

By the time John was removed from the Conservative Mennonite church he had acquired a small group of followers. Approximately twenty-five people left with him. All of them had either previously been Amish or Conservative Mennonite and they were just like John — hungry for truth, not tradition.

As they did not yet have a church building to meet in, Abner Yoder, also a dissident from the Amish and Conservative Mennonite church offered the use of his garage for their meetings. It wasn't long before that garage would no longer be big enough to house them all as now there were about forty-five people attending the meetings.

A couple that had also followed had a home on the main street of Shanesville, Ohio. They lived in the upstairs and the downstairs was a vacant storefront. This vacant storefront would become the next meeting place for the outcast band of believers.

It was here that John once again started to preach from the book of Acts:

> Acts 2:1–4 KJV, *"And when the day of Pentecost was fully come, they were all with one accord in one place. 2) And suddenly there came a sound from heaven as of a rushing mighty wind, and it filled all the house where they were sitting. 3) And there appeared unto them cloven tongues like as of fire, and it sat upon each of them. 4) And they were all filled with the Holy Ghost, and began to speak with other tongues, as the Spirit gave them utterance.*

At this service a woman stood up and said, "I am not leaving here until I am filled with the Holy Ghost." None of the congregants had ever known anyone who was filled with the Holy Ghost, but they experienced it in the book of Acts and these people were convinced that it was available. None of them knew what to do.

It just so happened that a stranger that was seated at the back of the church walked up front to pray for the woman. As he laid his hands on her and started to pray, suddenly she began speaking in tongues in her heavenly language and everyone there began shouting and praising God. God's word was real and this was the most evident display of His power that these people had seen to date. They believed the Bible as literal with childlike faith and the Holy Spirit showed up in a big way that night.

The stranger seated in the back of the church that night was a minister from Strasburg, Ohio. That evening he was told by God that he was to go to Shanesville. He had no idea why he was there. As he stopped for a red light on the corner very close to the store front where they were meeting, he heard people praising God. He decided to stop and attend the meeting as he did not know where else he was supposed to go. It wasn't long before he knew why God had compelled him to go to Shanesville.

Less than a week after the woman had been filled with the Holy Spirit, Marie (John's wife) was lying in bed reading a book. The only person in their group that was filled with the Holy Spirit at this point was the woman that the minister from Strasburg had prayed over. In Marie's mind she struggled a bit with doubt. As she was reading the book *Power from on High* every doubt she had was instantly removed. She found herself lying in bed speaking in tongues.

At this time Marie had four small children, the oldest

being around six years of age. She struggled to get out of bed and had an overwhelming feeling that she refers to as what it must feel like to be drunk. She stumbled as she could barely make her way to the door.

She yelled for Jo Ann (the oldest of the four children) to run over to where John was working, which was two doors down, and to ask him to come home immediately.

When John opened the bedroom door, he instantly knew that Marie had just had an encounter with the Holy Spirit.

When these happenings made their way throughout the community it was no longer just 80% of the people that were outraged. It was the entire community.

There are many Biblical scriptures that very clearly show the same types of accusations that were being made against these spirit-filled believers that were made against the disciples of Jesus.

Everything that these people were experiencing could be found and supported with Biblical scripture. But that didn't matter to the community. The bottom line was that it was not part of their teachings or traditions.

The following Sunday a pastor from a Holiness church in Florida was in the area. He had been informed of the goings on that were happening and he felt compelled to stop by to set the record and these people straight. He proceeded to tell them that what they were experiencing was wrong and that those teachings in the Bible were not for them today.

His words fell on deaf ears with the exception of three couples in attendance. The rest of the congregants were not swayed by what this man had to say. What they had witnessed the prior Sunday was real and the only thing that mattered to them was having that same experience themselves.

Unfortunately, the words spoken by this man, combined with the backlash from the community, weighed on the couple that had volunteered the building in which they were meeting. They were fearful of what they did not understand and had not yet experienced. They allowed their fear of the unknown and of the community to overtake them. They were no longer willing to allow the group to meet at their storefront.

Including the owners of the storefront, there were three couples that parted ways from the group when the Holy Spirit made Himself evident through speaking in tongues. It was time once again for them to find a new place to meet.

Next, they found an abandoned schoolhouse in Millersburg, Ohio, for their meetings. It was at this time that they knew a church building of their own would be necessary. As they were meeting in that schoolhouse, two of the congregants, Abner and Henry Yoder (brothers), both skilled craftsman, spearheaded the building of what I refer to as "the little white church."

It was at this abandoned school house where the presence of God showed up and showed off. Every congregant longed to be filled with the Holy Spirit and they were not disappointed. The Holy Spirit made His presence known in big ways.

One evening as the Holy Spirit fell during worship service, Fannie (Marie's mom), literally slid off of the church pew straight onto the floor. The next thing you know, the piano fell silent as the piano player slid off of the piano bench. Now she, too, was on the floor! Both women received the baptism of the Holy Spirit that night. The presence of God was so strong that many were unable to stand. No one was laying hands or even praying over them. They fell to the ground due solely to the strong and intoxicating presence of the Holy Spirit.

This move of God in Amish country was taking place at the same time as the Jesus People and Charismatic Renewal movements. Although the Amish are an isolated community, God broke through.

No one ever wanted to miss a service because you never knew what was going to happen. It didn't matter to any of them what the naysayers said. They knew they had found the truth and the truth was setting them free. And man, were they free.

In fact, they were so free that one night a neighbor to this abandoned schoolhouse called the police. They were convinced that something sinister was taking place in that school house.

The police visited one of the services without any of the congregants' knowledge and placed a microphone connected to a tape recorder through an open window. The police later reported back to the neighbor that filed the complaint. They told the neighbor "they might be crazy, but they are harmless."

Prior to the birthing of the little white church, God had prepared John for the role of pastor and teacher he was about to assume. God gave John a dream. In this dream John found himself alone on a desert island, surrounded by sand and one palm tree. In the sand he saw a book and as he picked up the book he noticed the title *The Book of Life*. John opened the book and it was, in fact, the Bible, but with one huge difference. While he read this book of life everything he had ever learned in his life had been removed. He was able to read this book with absolutely no preconceived ideas or teachings. His understanding as he read this book became completely pure.

As he read this book, he felt the emotions and experiences of every person he read about. If he was reading about Samson, it were as though he was Samson. When he read about Paul, it was as though he were Paul. This gave John an incredible understanding of the Bible. He didn't just know the scripture, he had lived the scripture through that dream.

Throughout John's adult life, everyone was always in awe of his Biblical knowledge and understanding. When John taught from the Bible no one would have ever guessed that he only had an 8th grade education and no formal theological training. His training and teaching truly came directly from God.

Upon completion of their new building, the little white church, Berlin Gospel Tabernacle, opened its doors towards the end of September in 1961.

This church was established as a non-denominational church, as none of them ever again wanted to be held back by Bible teachings that a denomination considered to be off limits. If it wasn't off limits in the Bible, it wasn't off limits at that church.

There were no membership requirements for the little white church attendees as John wanted everyone to come of their own free will and not out of obligation. He also wanted them to be free to leave without incident if they so chose. God gave people free will. John was certainly not going to take that away.

They did not focus on a list of things that were not allowed. They had lived that way for long enough.

Women were wearing dresses with prints and it wasn't long before they started to wear makeup and jewelry. These things were completely off-limits prior.

The community would refer to the little white church as "do ve do vit gmay" translated as "do as you please church."

The little white church was known throughout the community to house the misfits, the rejects and the sinners — you know all the kinds of people that churches are actually supposed to welcome in their doors. You didn't have to be perfect in order to be accepted. Everyone there was a work in progress.

There were no cliques in this church, there was only family. They did not put on airs or pretend to be something special, these were humble people that truly looked out and helped care for each other. After all, these people were pretty much all any of them had left since most of them were shunned or rejected by their own families.

John held the position of Pastor in the little white church. Initially John was teaching on things that none of them had yet experienced. As he taught, God moved and it wasn't long before there were many testimonies being shared that directly related to that teaching. God did not disappoint these people. He showed up in a big way in all of their lives.

John's preaching style was never that of hell fire and brimstone which was a very common style back in the 1960s. John did not view Christianity as a means to avoid hell, although no doubt that was a benefit of it. He viewed it as how to have life and how to live it more abundantly. He believed Christians should be the most successful and the happiest people on earth.

John's sermons seemed so simple and yet they packed a punch. Sermons that everyone could immediately use in their everyday life and these people's lives were starting to transform.

His teachings were unheard of back in those days and some of the props he used to get his points across were completely unconventional. You absolutely never knew what was going to happen at any given service.

One such service John hired an ambulance service to transport one of the congregants to the church. Upon arrival, the door to the church opened and the EMTs carted in the congregant on a stretcher.

John approached the congregant on the stretcher and pulled out a fishing pole, golf balls and many other recreational items. The point that he was making is that many people skip church to do those types of things. As time goes by, they soon find themselves sick — not sick of body, but sick spiritually. His sermons were filled with truth and yet delivered in a very entertaining and humorous way that stuck with you.

During the time that John was teaching on healing, his wife Marie had been suffering from a hernia. Up to that point no one in the church had experienced any supernatural healing. Once again, it was in the Bible and they believed it was available for them today.

John decided that he should pray for Marie to be healed. He laid his hands on her and tried to pray the kind of prayer that he felt might work. He tried to grab big fancy words and threw in a few "thus sayeth the Lords." Finally, he admitted defeat and cried out "Oh God" at which time both John and Marie started to laugh. As they were laughing uncontrollably Marie was instantly healed. It gave meaning to the scripture found in Proverbs 17:22 KJV, *"A merry heart doeth good like a medicine."*

Over time, the little white church people were operating in all of the gifts of the spirit. Sick people were healed, people were prophesying, people were dreaming dreams, others were having visions, there was interpretation of tongues and even dancing in the spirit. They made room for the Holy Spirit at every service and were delighted to follow His lead.

Acts 2:17 KJV, *"And it shall come to pass in the last days, saith God, I will pour out of my Spirit upon all flesh: and your sons and your daughters shall prophesy, and your young men shall see visions, and your old men shall dream dreams"*

Feet washing was also a common occurrence at the little white church. This act is virtually unheard of today. Looking back, for me, this was one of the most beautiful acts that I have ever witnessed and of which I have been a part. This teaching came from the book of John.

John 13:12–17 KJV, "*So after he had washed their feet, and had taken his garments, and was set down again, he said unto them, Know ye what I have done to you? Ye call me Master and Lord: and ye say well; for so I am. If I then, your Lord and Master, have washed your feet; ye also ought to wash one another's feet. For I have given you an example, that ye should do as I have done to you. Verily, verily, I say unto you, The servant is not greater than his lord; neither he that is sent greater than he that sent him. If ye know these things, happy are ye if ye do them.*"

Full emersion baptisms were performed in the Doughty Valley Creek on the same day that we had our church picnics. One such time in the early spring, the creek was starting to ice over. One of the congregants broke through the ice, and the baptisms took place. A little bit of ice wasn't going to stop them.

Witnessing these baptisms made it easy to visualize what baptisms might have been like back in Jesus's days.

Testimonies were a big part of every service. People freely stood to their feet and shared the many things that God had done for them and taken them through. These testimonies energized and fueled the congregants. Shouts of praise and glory to God would always follow.

Worship at the little white church was amazing. Worship leaders weren't necessarily the best singers, but they were exceptional at following the lead of the Holy Spirit. The congregants would accept anyone as a worship leader as long as they always made room for the Holy Spirit to flow. If they only followed their agenda then their time as worship leader would be very short. Congregants were there to worship, not to be entertained or to watch a performance. The songs were simple and they often sang them over and over again. *My God Can Do Anything, I've Taken My Harp Down, Let it Breathe on Me* and *There's a River of Life* are just a few examples. In between songs you would hear several minutes of people breaking out in song in their own heavenly language.

There are stories from out-of-towner's that drove by the little white church, upon hearing the worship they stopped to listen. Several people that stopped to listen insisted that they heard a choir of angels singing along in harmony with the congregants.

If the Holy Spirit was flowing they just went with it and they had no problem waiting for Him to show up.

There wasn't a strict structure to services, church was very informal — whatever God wanted to do — they made room for Him to do. There were services that went until 3 am and even some that lasted until sunrise. People that needed to leave felt free to do so, but the majority of the people stayed because they didn't want to miss out on what God was doing.

Instead of returning to their homes in between the morning and evening services on Sundays, many families would spend the day together at the church. Everyone was welcome to stay. There were many carry-in lunches served at the little white church. It was not uncommon to find people remaining for an hour and often times longer after any given service.

One time, as we as a family were driving by a building, my brother J.D. noticed people walking out of it. They were walking out in single file, one person right after the next. He asked my parents, "What are those people doing?" They replied, "Their church service must have just ended." This was inconceivable to J.D. as he had never seen anything like that before. When our church service ended, it was just the beginning of the time we would all spend together. No one was ever sprinting out the door to leave.

There were little to no politics in the little white church. John was the only person that held a pastor's title. Every other position was filled by people that volunteered. Everyone was welcome to participate in any capacity. John encouraged people to step out and help in ministry. He wanted to see people grow in their gifts. He knew that in order for that to happen, they needed the freedom and experience to do so. Regardless if it was teaching Sunday school, leading worship, playing music or if you were featured singing during the offering — people were encouraged to step out. Some people were better than others. But regardless of the level of talent, everyone at the church supported them. Over time, many became incredibly gifted in their role.

Over the years, many evangelists that had heard about this little white church eventually made their way to this little Amish community. One such evangelist and his family ministered at the church several times over the years. These people soon became good friends with John and his family.

They invited John and Marie on a trip to the Holy Land. After visiting the Holy Land, they extended their trip to visit 18 additional countries for their ministry and invited John to share his testimony. At that time, John believed that this completed the fulfillment of the first thing that God told him would happen in his life — that he would be a minister and travel the world giving his testimony. Unbeknownst to John, this was only the beginning of the fulfillment of that prophecy.

John continued to pastor this church for the next thirteen years. He never received a salary or any type of payment from the church. Actually, it was quite the contrary when, in fact, he was one of the biggest financial contributors. Pastoring this church when there were services every Sunday morning, Sunday evening and Wednesday evening was quite a feat. John was also working 60+ hours a week at his own business. But he was always available, always committed and always willing to do whatever was necessary.

People's lives were truly transformed in every possible way. Those people that had entered as rejects or had wounds from sin of their own or from other religious groups found teaching filled with truth that set them free. This church did not attract leaders — this church developed leaders. Many of the members from the little white church are today highly regarded within the same communities that had rejected and mocked them. Success in life is hard to deny. The seeds that

God planted in these people germinated and repopulated all over the world. What greater evidence could there ever be of a move of God than that?

To this day, all of the people that attended the little white church will tell you the same story — they have never found another church that has ever even come close to what they were fortunate enough to experience at Berlin Gospel Tabernacle.

By the early 1980's the little white church was packed to capacity and a new church was built.

Prior to them moving into this new building, John saw the sign in the sky that God had told him to watch for. This sign was to let him know that the Kingdom prophecy God had spoken to him regarding the Spirit of Elijah being released on earth had been fulfilled and now the 3rd prophetic event in John's life had also been fulfilled.

Today that little white church matured into Berlin Christian Fellowship, located one mile west of Berlin, Ohio. John remained a faithful member and the senior elder at BCF throughout his life.

"If there were no heaven or hell, I'd still live this way — because it works."

—John E. Schrock

"*Christianity is life. Real life. You don't have to wait till you die to get to heaven. You can have that right here and right now. I believe it will make your life work. Your life will blossom and bloom. Your life will be like the prophets of old and those great patriotic leaders, who were anointed by God to do signs, miracles and wonders. I believe that's it! I am uneducated, I don't claim to be smart. I'm just a man that believes in God and believes in truth and that has made my life work.*"

—John E. Schrock

CHAPTER FOUR

Music Days

As you've already discovered in the previous chapters, John had a major love of country and gospel music. That love of music never ceased throughout his life.

To John, the songs were all about the lyrics, be it country music or gospel. If the lyrics conveyed the heart of God, he loved the song.

The little white church was also unusual due to the number of musicians that honed and perfected their craft within its walls. Music and worship, as you know, were a huge part of the little white church's story.

In the 1960s, right smack dab in the middle of Amish country, at any given church service, you'd find guitars of all types, a piano, an organ, drums, tambourines — if it made music, you'd find it there. You'd also find the congregants often times playing together for hours after the service had ended.

In 1964, John and one of the congregants (and personal

friend), Lee Swartzentruber, started a band. They were known as Johnny and Lee. They launched their first album in 1965 called *This Little Light of Mine.*

Their style was very much like that of the Louvin Brother's, including Lee's talent in playing a variety of styles on his mandolin. Lee also had an unusually fine tenor voice.

Johnny and Lee traveled with their band performing in various venues throughout the state of Ohio and in neighboring states.

In the mid-1960s, they also had their own radio show that aired on WTOF out of Canton, Ohio, called "Gospel Echoes with Johnny and Lee."

It was during these days that John Ruth was recruited to play in Johnny and Lee's band. John Ruth was already playing for a country music group at the time, but agreed to play with them.

For over a year, John Ruth attended every practice held at the little white church and traveled with them to every performance. One day John Ruth asked John why he had never asked him to come to church. John replied, "I thought if you like what you see you'll come." John Ruth replied ,"I'll come if I can bring my guitar."

John Ruth did, in fact, start attending the little white church. He brought his guitar and a whole new level of musical talent with him.

In his early music days, John Ruth's talent as a musician was so great that he was pursued by the country music industry. He was offered a very lucrative position within the

Grand Ole Opry in Nashville, Tennessee. Ultimately, he declined, but I am noting it to give you a glimpse of the level of musical talent that you could find in the little white church.

John Ruth was an exceptional electric and steel guitarist but his greatest musical accomplishment was yet to come. John actually learned how to play piano because the little white church had a need.

The previous piano player had moved to Mexico to work as a nanny for a missionary family. The church needed a piano player, so John Ruth said he'd give it a shot. He was self-taught and played by ear. His style was very much like that of Floyd Cramer and his talent is every bit as great. To this day, nothing says, "I'm home," and nothing takes me back to the little white church days like when I hear the roar of his piano playing.

As the years passed, John's wife Marie would find herself singing harmony with John. They recorded several albums together as well. *From the Heart of Amish Country* and *One Day at a Time* to name a couple.

John wrote and recorded five songs of his own. His first was "Eternity" and how it affected him. Then came "When The Sun Refused To Shine," a song about the facts of the future. "Pioneer Days" was written for the annual pioneer days celebration held in Berlin, Ohio. "Bring it to Jesus" is an expression of loneliness for the Savior in the time of disappointment. "He is Mine" was his last and his favorite.

Another venture that John headed up was to bring country and gospel music performers to a venue in Berlin, Ohio. John rented the high school gymnasium for these events. He would bring in up-and-coming talents from the country music scene as well as recruit local and well-known gospel music groups to perform. They were a big deal back in those days and every single one was packed to capacity.

The most interesting part that I remember is the number of Amish young people in attendance. You would find them not only at these concerts, but in nearly all of the venues Johnny and Lee performed in. It is distinctly possible that the Amish and Conservative Mennonites were among Johnny and Lee's greatest fans.

There were seasons in John's life that allowed him to revert back to his love of music. His final years were no exception. After retirement, John once again teamed up with another gentleman from the community, and cousin to Marie, Floyd Mullet. John and Floyd sang and performed at various venues locally and also in the surrounding states.

Together, they recorded several CDs in addition to establishing an annual gospel music concert that takes place every fall at Berlin Christian Fellowship. This event continues to be held annually.

Late in his life new voices emerged within the Amish and Mennonite communities. Many of whom shared with John that he was their inspiration. John's God-inspired love of music paved the way for many to come.

Throughout John's life, his love of music never wavered.

CHAPTER FIVE

Entrepreneur Days

The second of the four things that God had told John would happen in his life would that he would become a businessman. Once again, God was true to His word.

In 1957, John and Marie were residing in Sugarcreek, Ohio. Marie had given birth to their second child. Not long after the birth of this child, their first son, they discovered that he was born with a defect in his heart. The doctors told them that their son would not survive the Ohio winter if he so much as caught a cold. They immediately packed up their bags and headed to Florida for the winter.

Upon arrival in Florida, John went in search of a job. He stopped by a gas and service station in the hopes that they were hiring. The owner said that he had no job openings but he did know of another gas and service station that was hiring. John immediately went to apply.

The owner of the establishment went by Cookie. Cookie

inquired about John's qualifications to work at his business. Cookie asked John if he knew how to change oil and John replied, "No." He asked John if he knew how to change a tire and John replied, "No." He asked, "Have you ever tuned up a car?" Again, John replied, "No." John explained to him that he had only recently started to drive a car and that he grew up Amish and the Amish mode of transportation was horse and buggy.

Cookie asked why should he consider hiring him. John replied, "Because I'm a hard worker. I'm honest. I'm a Christian and I believe that I can learn."

Cookie shook his head and chuckled. John saw the doubt in Cookie's response.

John made an offer to Cookie that was impossible to refuse. John told Cookie that he would work the first two weeks for free. At the end of the two weeks, if Cookie felt that John had earned a paycheck, then at that time he could pay him and officially hire him.

Who wouldn't take someone up on an offer like that? John believed in himself, he knew he was willing to work hard and to learn.

After the two weeks were up, Cookie opened the cash drawer and paid John in cash for those two weeks of work. Cookie was very happy with his work and John was hired full time for the duration of their time in Florida.

John's willingness to work hard, his willingness to take a risk and sacrifice himself and his willingness to prove himself got him a job. Not only did it get him a job but this experience led John into something far greater that he did not foresee.

Village Gulf Days–1960s

Upon returning to Ohio in the spring, John had an oil leak in his car. He stopped by the Gulf service station in Berlin to ask if he could use their rack to check out his car. The station owner said he didn't normally allow people to do things like that because it was not safe for people that don't know how to operate the rack.

John responded that he had just returned from Florida where he had been working for a service station and that he was well-trained in the procedure. Soon the owner agreed to allow John to use the rack.

After a bit the owner said to John, "So you just returned from Florida. Are you looking for a job?" John replied, "Well, I guess I am." The owner proceeded to tell John that he had just been diagnosed with the mumps and that he would like to hire John to run the business for two weeks until he fully recovered.

John agreed to the challenge and with only an hour or two of training he was charged with operating this business. Over the course of the next two weeks, John needed to call the owner for help only one or two times. This led to John's full-time employment at the Gulf station.

One day, the owner said to John, "You love this business much more than I do. Everyone is coming in and asking for you. You serve and take better care of my customers than I do. Are you at all interested in buying this business?" John replied, "Well I don't know, I don't really have any money to buy it but I would be willing to see if we can work something out."

They did, in fact, work out a deal that was fair to them both and it wasn't long until John became the new owner of The Village Gulf station in Berlin, Ohio.

This purchase took place during the same time the little white church was being built in Berlin. Since all of his time was now being spent in Berlin, John soon purchased a home there.

This opportunity of becoming the owner of the Gulf station would not have presented itself if John had not been initially willing to work for free. He worked hard and he proved his value. John would often say, "Work is plentiful, but you have to earn the right to get paid." Now not only was he getting paid, he was starting to build his own wealth by becoming a business owner.

This Gulf station located in a horse-and-buggy town went from one of Gulf Corporations smallest revenue franchises to one of their top performing franchises in the state within five years under John's ownership.

The Gulf corporation was amazed at the results. They asked John how he was able to accomplishing this in a horse-and-buggy town. John replied, "Because I am known far and wide throughout the state of Ohio to have the ability to fix anything, including holes in gas tanks. When people bring their cars in for repair, they fill up with gas." To John, it was that simple.

As I was writing this story, the Bible scripture found in 1 Corinthians 1:27 continued to run through my mind. *"But God chose the foolish things of the world to shame the wise; God chose the weak things of the world to shame the strong."*

John grew up Amish with only an eighth grade education. He was rejected, mocked and told he would never amount to anything. It really didn't matter what man had to say about John, as God would have the final word.

God gifted John with the ability to fix any vehicle — when John's own mode of transportation had been horse and buggy for nearly his entire life.

Many people that had once said that John wouldn't amount to anything in life and that had even mocked him, found themselves with no option but to take their vehicles to John for repair.

John certainly was not an educated man. However, he was gifted with common sense. He learned from every experience in his life. He analyzed both the things that worked and the things that didn't work and he was building an arsenal of knowledge a formal education could never have provided him with.

"Not everything in life is a blessing from God. Some things are earned."

—John E. Schrock

Mini Merchant, Homes Guide, & Freeport Press Days — 1970-1980s

In 1971, when John was 40 years of age, he approached Marie and informed her that she needed to cut back on expenses. God had told John that He was about to lead him into a major life change.

Without knowing where or what God had in store for him, John sold the Village Gulf station to one of his workers, just as the previous owner had done for him. John simply believed God and he was now waiting for his next big adventure.

In 1972, God used John Ruth, the same man that had previously performed with Johnny & Lee, to lead five men chosen by God to John's side. There is no doubt that John was about to encounter a divine appointment.

John Ruth had been involved in a network marketing motivation program and had been relocated to West Virginia as this company had closed the Ohio territory. After a short time in West Virginia, John Ruth became homesick and felt compelled to return to Ohio. His first stop was to see John.

As John Ruth shared with John the happenings in his life and the program he had just left, John immediately recognized this as the set-up to the new thing that God had been stirring in John's heart. This stirring in John was to develop a program that would help churches grow leaders. John knew this was God at work, and he literally did somersaults out of excitement.

Over the next six months, John and John Ruth worked relentlessly to put together a program called Dynamic Living. Dynamic Living was a set of teachings based upon values and principles from the Bible that if applied properly, would transform lives.

Unfortunately, they soon discovered that churches were rejecting Dynamic Living as the program was designed more for those who were already leaders than for the average congregant. They were not rejected because they were theologically incorrect. They were rejected because churches could not figure out how to apply them.

John Ruth felt compelled to introduce John to the five other men that he had been involved with in the network marketing program. Unbeknownst to John Ruth at the time, God used him to set up this divine appointment.

The kingdom of God is all about collaboration, and God never does anything without telling his prophets first. After this initial meeting of these seven men had taken place, a divine collaboration was about to be set into motion by God.

One of the men, Ernie Blood, had been given a divine mission by God to set up a training center to help sales people be ethical representatives. He called this the Universal Training Center (UTC). Ernie sent out invitations to the same five men which included John Ruth. John, invited by John Ruth, was unable to attend the meeting but a providential relationship was about to take place.

At this meeting Ernie cast the vision of the training center. John Ruth then shared with the group the program that John had developed called Dynamic Living. At this time, these two seeds of the Universal Training Center and Dynamic Living came together. God was about to show that Dynamic Living was more than a philosophy. It would be a program that worked providentially in the business arena.

When God told John that his life was about to undergo a major change, He certainly did not disappoint. These six men were incredibly dynamic and charismatic men. They drove big flashy Cadillacs, wore mink ties and wild vibrant suits. Several were divorced, several smoked, several had even been involved in the 1960's hippie movement. One of them, Bob, performed with Stephen Stills from the group Crosby, Stills & Nash.

Seeing John with these men was indeed a sight to behold. In appearance, this should have been an epic fail. God could not have possibly sent men into John's life that were of greater contrast to John's conservative values. And yet somehow it worked. These men all needed each other.

The other members of the group had also fallen victim to the same things that John Ruth had encountered with the previous network marketing venture. This encounter with John and Dynamic Living was like a breath of fresh air to all of them. The truth they were hearing drew them in and they wanted more.

There was an instant bond and camaraderie between these seven men. As much as they all wanted to work together to promote Dynamic Living and UTC, knowing that it would require years to get it off the ground, they also knew that in the meantime they needed to make a living.

In an effort to keep them connected they decided to invest in real estate and meet once a week to stay encouraged.

Their first mastermind meeting was held in Columbus, Ohio. It was at this meeting that the idea was given on how they could begin a publishing business rather than a real estate business.

In 1973, Mini Merchant was founded with offices located in Canton, Ohio. Mini Merchant was a classified, "pay when and if you sell" newspaper type of publication that covered seven counties.

After only six months, they found themselves on the brink of having to admit defeat. The expenses were far exceeding their income. The only way for the business to survive was for the owners to invest additional money to keep it going. This is when John discovered that all six of these men were flat broke. One of the partners brought in a consultant in hopes that he could steer them in the right direction. The consultant's terms would be to receive partial ownership of the business.

This just made no sense to John. He believed in what they were doing, he saw the potential in this team and in the business, itself.

Up until that time, all of the decisions made were made by the team. John's role and his voice was one of seven. John made a proposal to the team. He would make arrangements for the financing of the business ,but he wanted to be in charge to lead them and to make the final decisions.

Unlike the proposal from the consultant, this would allow each of them to continue to have the same percentage of ownership they had prior. John had a proven success record in business under his belt and was willing to take the risk.

However, there was one additional proposal that John made to the team. John stated that there was one thing they had not done. He said, "We need to dedicate this company to the Lord, to His work and to bring honor and glory to Him. That is what is needed to be done if we truly want to be successful." He asked each person if they were in agreement of dedicating it to God.

Although most of these men were not saved at the time, and more than likely didn't even know what those words meant, each partner agreed. They joined hands and prayed and committed the company to the Lord. From that day forward every meeting they held began and ended with prayer.

Within six months under John's leadership, this business that they committed to God experienced a real, true miracle. Things started to turn around and the numbers started to increase and everything started to work. The favor of God was now with them.

It wasn't long after this that two of the partners decided that they would prefer to operate their own businesses. The partners negotiated a buyout leaving five partners remaining: John Schrock, Bernie Torrence, John Ruth, Ernie Blood, and Bob Harmelink.

In 1978, Bernie asked John where he could find the best Biblical training and teaching for success in their business. John told Bernie to read and study the book of Proverbs.

Not only did Bernie read and study it, but he also put the

information together in a small book form that he could hand out to others. He kept a copy with him at all times. This book was called "The Principles of Proverbs." It became their go-to reference for Bernie and the team throughout this venture.

In time, the remaining partners added an additional publication — Foto Tab, which eventually would be part of the Auto Trader magazines.

Additionally, in 1978, the workers at the Canton Repository newspaper went on strike. This left the Realtors with very few options to showcase their listings to potential buyers. Their need would be filled by the team's introduction of the Homes Guide magazines.

Homes Guide was a photo magazine for Realtors to showcase their listings. If you were looking to buy a house, you had access to pictures of all the homes available in your area including a description, just by picking up one of these free magazines.

Now keep in mind, these are the days before the internet. While there were other magazines that were published monthly or every other week, the Homes Guide magazine was published weekly and offered free open house listings as well as free new listings. These magazines provided a huge value to the Realtors as well as to anyone considering purchasing a new home. Before long they found themselves opening additional locations across the United States. Within 10 years, they had taken these publications nationwide, servicing the needs of 12,000 Realtors in 55 cities across the country. They established six graphic centers across the United States and were employing close to 900 people.

Not only did they provide an invaluable resource to Realtors through their Homes Guide Magazines, they also provided them with outstanding sales training for the Realtors themselves.

This organization grew into one of the largest publication and training organizations in the United States. They trained literally tens of thousands of salespeople and managers. Wherever they saw a need, they stepped in to fill that need. This led to huge success for them.

In 1985, the owner of Freeport Press propositioned the Homes Guide team regarding a potential partnership. For years, Freeport Press's business was heavily dependent upon the Homes Guide printing business. This gentleman believed that his best option of maintaining Homes Guide's printing would be to go into partnership with this team.

The partners discussed it and agreed to the proposal. Once again each of them became equal partners in this new venture. Each of them invested $3,333.33 to buy into the partnership with Freeport Press.

Several of the remaining five partners had begun attending the little white church. As new Christians they brought a whole new culture and excitement to the little white church and were loved and adored everywhere they went. They had all become men of principles and values. God had transformed their hearts, minds and their entire lives as a result.

The success of these men and their commitment to tithing to the little white church was hugely instrumental in the little white church's ability to build a new and bigger facility.

Everyone who knew these men will tell you the same story. They always gave all the credit, honor and glory to God for their success. They knew without a doubt where their success came from and they were never shy about sharing their love of Jesus with everyone that they came into contact with.

In early 1988, due to Homes Guide's visible success in the marketplace, John and the team were approached by the Hartz Mountain Company regarding a potential acquisition of all of the publications. Shortly afterwards, they received an offer from Leonard Stern to purchase. Leonard Stern was the chairman and CEO of the privately-owned Hartz Group located in New York City. He was one of the richest men in the United States at that time.

This offer was substantial and it gave the remaining four partners cause to consider. One of the five previous partners, John Ruth, had sold his shares earlier due to personal issues that needed attention.

After much deliberation, they all agreed to the offer. They had accomplished more than they could have ever believed as it was. By this time, John was in his late 50's and ready for a change. He was the only one who was more than ready to sell — he was no doubt the driving force of the sale.

The sale was final in 1988 and the four remaining partners became millionaires. God had been working overtime in all of their lives and in these businesses for fifteen years. It was time to close this chapter of the book and for a new chapter to begin.

Unbeknownst to them, it wouldn't be long before the

publishing industry would very quickly undergo great changes due to the introduction of new technology. Major equipment investments that they had made would have proven to be burdensome and outdated. God in His goodness, protected them and they sold these publications at the peak of the market.

Shortly after the sale of the Homes Guide magazines, John approached the team and informed them that there were some major issues happening at Freeport Press that needed to be addressed. However, John knew there was huge financial risk involved in doing so. John made it clear to the team what the risks were.

In addition to the problems they were already encountering at the printing plant, the new owners of Homes Guide were getting quotes from other companies for their printing needs. This left everyone feeling even more insecure. At this time each team member decided to sell their shares of Freeport Press to John. Each of them received $200,000 for their shares. That made for an incredible return on investment in a little over four years.

But now John carried all of the risk for this business himself. This was the biggest risk in John's business ventures to date. John, unable to be on site daily, needed to find the right person to oversee it.

Once again, God did not leave John disappointed. God had the right man for the job tucked away for such a time as this. This man was not only hired to run the entire facility, but he also had a vested interest in its success as he had also purchased a minority share of the company.

This man had full knowledge of the obstacles that needed to be overcome and believed strongly that he could lead them through it.

Freeport Press flourished under this man's leadership. John was able to maintain this partnership with very little of his time dedicated towards it which allowed him the freedom to venture into other businesses.

The Freeport Press venture was by far John's greatest success to date as this business was asset heavy. John's willingness to risk it all would pay off in a big way in the future. God's timing would show superb.

Holmes Progressive Developers (HPD) Days — 1990's

For the fifteen years that John worked in Canton, his home remained in Berlin. During the Mini Merchant/Homes Guide days he commuted the 40 miles between Berlin and Canton on a daily basis. He enjoyed the two hours of commute time each day. It gave John time to gather his thoughts and prepare for his day as well as the opportunity to unwind prior to his return home for the evening.

John was always a country boy at heart, despite having traveled the world. Berlin was home to him and even with all of this newfound success and wealth he had no desire to relocate.

John was not driven or motivated by money or material possessions. He was a visionary and in order to fulfill those visions money was a necessity.

Despite the way that John had been treated by the community — having been shunned, excommunicated and rejected — it never changed John's love for this community. He didn't see the bad. Instead, he realized how much good there was in many of the ways this community operated.

He realized that they operated in values and principles without thought. These things were planted in children throughout their lives, not through some sort of school or training program provided for them. The parents modeled these things for their children.

A person's word and a handshake are their contract.
Principle of Dependability

They are outstanding stewards of their land,
homes and possessions.
Principle of Ownership

There was literally no crime in the area. Back in those days people left their houses unlocked and the keys in their cars.
Principle of Honesty

They weren't just farmers, they were also builders and extraordinary craftsmen. Their quality standard was based to withstand generational use.
Principle of Proper Thinking

They were willing to pay the price for the benefit of future generations.

Principle of Effective Planning

Divorce was nearly none existent.

Principle of Resolving Conflict

If anything bad happened to anyone — the loss of a loved one, a fire, an accident or any need amongst the community — every community member jumped in to help.

Principle of Generosity

Nearly all of their food came from their own farms. They were a very self-sufficient community.

Principle of Sowing

Their work ethic was second to none.

Principle of Hard Work

In the event that someone did cross a line or break a rule no police or judges would be necessary. The community swiftly dealt with these people. *(I'm not saying necessarily that it was always the right way, but I will make a case for the fact that you thought twice before doing something wrong. You had full knowledge of what was in store for you in the event that you got caught.)*

Principle of Chastisement/Correction

Under no circumstances were they relying on the government to take care of them or provide them with anything. They took care of their own.

Principle of Responsibility

Health insurance was provided by the church from a fund
set aside from monies they all had paid into for tithing.
Doctor visits were rare for the Amish and considered a
last resort. They had home remedies for nearly every
ailment that were handed down for generations.

Principle of Saving

John realized that this community beautifully represented
what the world could look like utilizing a Kingdom operating
system.

He also knew that, in time, in a world filled with busyness,
people would long for the simplicity of the past. The Amish
lifestyle could not have better represented that.

In typical John Schrock visionary fashion, in 1987, he
had developed a big picture for a piece of property that he
purchased one mile west of Berlin.

Even prior to the sale of the publishing company, he had
already begun to build what it was that he was envisioning.

John had sold a portion of this land to the little white
church several years prior. That piece of property became the
new home to Berlin Christian Fellowship in 1985.

The businesses that John was about to build would be
constructed adjacent to the new church. By this time in John's
life, his reputation had become known for everything that he
touched turned to gold.

John and two other men held the majority of ownership;
however, they also opened up this new project and made it

available to the local people to invest in if they felt so inclined.

John truly wanted this to benefit the entire community. He believed if people had a vested interest they would be more apt to frequent the businesses.

The first business John built was a 300-seat restaurant with banquet rooms to accommodate an additional 300 guests.

The restaurants in the area were all serving traditional Amish comfort food such as chicken, roast beef, mashed potatoes and gravy. John wanted this restaurant to provide the local people with a greater variety of options, while still maintaining and serving traditional Amish dishes.

Next, he built a fitness center for the community. It included an Olympic-sized indoor swimming pool, racquetball courts, aerobic equipment and a weight room. His intent was only to break even with this business. His heart was to provide a currently non-existent resource for the community members.

The third and final construction was a 50 room, country style hotel. John believed, "If we build it they will come," meaning that he believed in time that Berlin would become a tourist destination. John coined the phrase, "From the Heart of Amish Country," as it was the name of one of his early record albums. Now that same phrase would once again come into play and be used when promoting tourism in Berlin, Ohio.

From the very beginning, this development was a struggle in every way possible. The costs to build far exceeded the estimates. Two of the three businesses to be built were among the top listed failure risks in the country — the restaurant and the fitness center. His businesses were not the exception to that rule.

Upon completion, John was able to hold them together through the recruitment of family members and some exceptionally talented team members. There were several years that these businesses, in fact, generated a significant amount of profit.

However, just the nature of these businesses always made them a struggle. Each business required people who were willing to basically give up their lives to make them successful.

These businesses were also open on Sunday. John felt strongly regarding that. He believed this would provide a much-needed service to the community. John's decision to open their doors on Sunday was a bold one. This resolution greatly limited these businesses' ability to hire and retain staff as the majority of the community still considered it a sin to work on Sunday. Interestingly enough, they didn't seem to have a problem patronizing them on Sundays.

In 1989, John purchased an Amish farm located one mile east of Berlin. He turned this farm into a working farm that tourists could walk through and learn about the Amish way of life. After all, the Amish were certainly not going to be sharing those ways. They were still, at that time, very much removed from the outside world and certainly were not going to be involved in tourism.

In the late 1990's, John also acquired four additional businesses and went into partnership on three more. He went from one opportunity to the next. John had accomplished all of this within about a ten-year time span.

In 2006, John took a hit that he did not foresee. One of

the businesses he went into partnership with came crashing down. Not a small crash, but a large crash.

It was discovered that his partner had been using company funds for his own major personal expenses and had not paid the federal payroll taxes for years. John had kept this business afloat for years by feeding it money from his own pocket, only to discover that the money was being used fraudulently. This had been the one business that refused to allow the books, the payroll, the payables, the financial statements to be handled by the corporate offices that had been set up for all of the businesses. Looking back, it is easy to see why this partner refused to allow it.

I am purposely not mentioning the name of the person or the business that created this nightmare as that is not what this book is about. I would not want to be the judge or the jury for any of this. I am just sharing the absolute truth and facts of the matter.

This was when the risk John had taken earlier with Freeport Press paid off. Over time, John had worked out a buyout agreement of his ownership shares with the same gentleman that he had recruited to run the entire facility. This would provide the cash flow needed for John to clean up this mess and to keep the bankers satisfied.

After the markets had contracted by late 2007 and the great recession began, John took another unanticipated hit. The market crash placed additional pressure on the businesses as they all instantly dropped in value. Bankers throughout the United States were living in fear of their potential losses with every business — not just with John's. The pressure that John found himself under was nearly unbearable.

Fortunately, a friend of John's and a ministry partner stepped in to help. John had helped Jerry Anderson out of a business situation he had previously been in and now Jerry was stepping in to help John. Jerry purchased HPD (restaurant, hotel and fitness center) at a fair price to Jerry and at a price that enabled John to clear up his financial obligation with the bank. This was nothing short of an answer to prayer for John.

Presently, Jerry has truly transformed these businesses into the most beautiful resort and destination by any person's standards. The grounds are spectacular with rock waterfalls, walking paths, a gazebo, pond and the most adorable children's village. The hotel rooms range from luxurious to affordable for anyone and are perfect accommodations for retreats, training seminars and weddings. Today they are known as Berlin Resort. For those interested check it out at www.berlinresort.net. Today, you will find Schrock's Heritage Village, one mile east of Berlin Ohio. Here you will find signs on the outside of each building that contain various principles written by John himself. Inside, you will find information regarding the story of John's life as well as the history of the property.

In Schrock's Heritage Village, you will find many unique shops, including one of the most spectacular Christmas stores in the United States, Tis The Season.

Coming soon you will find one of John's greatest desires for the area. After selling a portion of the land to local residents that shared the same dream as John's, a hotel and theatre are now under construction, opening their doors in 2018.

For more information regarding Schrock's Heritage Village check out www.amishfarmvillage.com.

Today, Berlin is a destination referred to as the Heart of Amish country. What John had envisioned has become a reality. I left there in 2007 and I am amazed at the transformation that has taken place in such a short period of time.

Even I, who cringes at the thought of tourism, must admit that I enjoy visiting it today as a tourist. The shops are unique, the town of Berlin is still quaint. The Amish community is very much involved in the tourism industry, which adds even more to the experience.

As brutal as those days were for John to survive, in the end, his life once again became plain and simple. It was not because he didn't have money or a good quality of life, but because he did in fact finish well. He was no longer a slave to his own need to create and build.

I, myself, have pondered and studied what appeared to me to be John's insatiable need of acquiring businesses over that fifteen-year time span.

Remember, he did not live lavishly or believe in a luxurious lifestyle. He allowed an indulgence for his family by putting in a swimming pool for his grandkids.

He was still living in the same house he bought back in the 1960s. So, what was it? What could possibly have been his driving force?

Having had a front-seat view of most of his business life I have developed a theory. I cannot make this claim as fact. I also did not come up with it because of this book. This theory was developed along the way as I watched him firsthand.

I believe John's driving force regarding the businesses in Berlin had arisen from a need to be validated and vindicated of the accusations made against him from the community in his early days. Allow me to elaborate a bit on this issue.

The community this happened in is the same community that had rejected, ridiculed and mocked him. Not only that, but he was also told he was going to hell, his children were going to hell and that he would never amount to anything.

Although John kept his head high and refused to focus on anything that was being said, it had to have an effect on him. I am his child, and I know what kind of effect it had on me. This absolutely had to have an effect on John if not consciously then subconsciously. To me, nothing else makes any sense. We all have weaknesses. None of us are perfect and we are all products of the events in our lives.

Never did I hear my dad speak ill of this community. He loved this community, he loved his Amish relatives and he was grateful for the background that God had given him.

As I have also now extensively studied the office of a prophet and how God operates in them, I have also come to the conclusion that John did not realize that everything he saw was perhaps not meant for him to personally accomplish.

My father's business life could not be separated from his spiritual life. While he experienced both success and failure in the business arena, there is no question that in God's record book it is all recorded as Kingdom success.

CHAPTER SIX

Kingdom Days: The Net

For nearly twenty years, John belonged to a Christian Businessmen's organization and served as an International Director. His involvement with this ministry began in the early 1970's.

This Christian ministry was testimony-based. As this ministry grew, it catered to celebrities, professional athletes, highly-visible ministers and successful businessmen. These people were then recruited as guest speakers at their meetings as they shared their inspirational testimonies.

In time, some people were elevated over others. Some member's expenses were paid for and others weren't. Favors, politics, networking and all that goes with that territory soon infiltrated this ministry.

John and many others were becoming disillusioned with the way this ministry was operating and the decisions they were making.

One such notable time was when this ministry was building a new headquarters in California. In the typical John Schrock fashion, he challenged this decision. John said, "You teach a doctrine that California is going to fall into the ocean and then you build a $3M building." I'm sure you know how well that statement was received.

But the final straw for John happened as the leader of this ministry was preparing to retire. The leader announced that his son would be replacing him.

This was inconceivable to John. He believed that a ministry position was an appointment from God, not based upon a family bloodline.

John was not alone in his thoughts on this matter. In 1989, John resigned his position with this organization as did an additional 30 International Directors.

These 30 ex-International Directors all believed that God was calling them to a new thing. Not knowing what that was and believing that God would lead them into it, they held a meeting in August 1989, in St. Louis, Missouri.

The first day of the meeting was long and no conclusions were reached. They were disappointed that day, knowing that God was calling them to this and yet He had not yet made Himself and His plan known to them.

They adjourned the meeting with prayer and asked each person to pray that night prior to sleep. Perhaps God would give one of them directions in a dream.

John was exhausted and went to bed immediately upon returning to his hotel room.

He woke up in the middle of the night to voices of what he thought were coming from the hallway or the room next to him.

A bit irritated by the interruption of his sleep, he decided to get up and make a trip to the restroom. As he made his way back to his bed, his vision became blurry and one of the voices became loud. He was about to see into a meeting in heaven through a vision. As he got his bearings, he grabbed a pen and paper and started to take notes.

He saw two men and he heard the words "bring forth the agenda". A large scroll was unrolled and stopped at a place towards the end called "Today in Time."

God then spoke and said, "It is time! I have men of vision, not plagued by former things. They will have an insight into my agenda.

They will be men of valor; fearless, bold and aggressive. They will look like lions, but have hearts like lambs.

These men and women will attract and find favor with great leaders of our time.

My agenda is already understood by many; however, it is understood more by national and political leaders than the religious.

They will be a new breed of a different spirit; confident and strong, yet gentle. They will be unmovable. Strength mixed with gentleness. Loving and caring. They will not appear to be super religious or over spiritual.

These men will be moved by the agenda. They will walk

*on earth as men of destiny, problem solvers, pace-setters,
operating in wisdom, motivated by My agenda, not seeking
the approval of the former."*
    *God then said; "the next years will involve major
changes. The world kingdoms will deteriorate and there will
be a rise of Christianity worldwide. The world will come to
Christians for answers".*

The next morning, John shared this vision with the group.
Everyone was excited, as you would imagine. God had not
disappointed them as they now had very clear direction from
God Himself.

It was at this time and at these meetings that these 30
men formed the International Fellowship of Christian
Businessmen's organization, (IFCB).

Their mission would be to train and develop Christian
leadership for this time of change.

The scope and reach of the relationships that these 30
International Directors had built over the last twenty years was
vast. This new organization hit the ground running and grew
rapidly in number.

John was put in charge of the training portion for this
organization. It would not be long before John reached out to
Bernie Torrence to help work on IFCB's monthly publication.
Bernie and John had just sold the publishing company where
he and John had been partners. This freed up Bernie's schedule
to dedicate a large portion of his time to the Kingdom of God.

It was during this time with IFCB that John first wrote

the principles in an individual format that businessmen could easily reference to find the Biblical solutions when encountering problems in their businesses.

These were the same principles that John and his team had built their success on in their own businesses but in a different format.

John and Bernie's relationships from their Homes Guide days would once again be called upon and prove to be very beneficial. However, this time it would be for the benefit of IFCB.

John and Bernie called on Lloyd Meredith, an old team member who had been highly instrumental in helping the Homes Guide team train thousands of sales people. John and Bernie called upon Lloyd to create a series of seminars called "The Challenge of Change."

The topics were *The Challenge of Team Building, The Challenge of Communication, The Challenge of Time Mastery, and The Challenge of Leadership.* This initial series served as the foundation for them to build upon.

God also was clarifying the vision that He had given to John. God showed John that He was restoring the plumb line in His Kingdom operating system. This system would be set up in a format to share Godly principles.

Shortly after this, God also gave John revelation for a new training methodology in a Roundtable format.

IFCB's format changed from a seminar-based format to a Roundtable Training Organization. As John shared with them one evening "line upon line and precept upon precept, we will be changed."

As this businessmen's organization was flourishing, soon a group of women discovered the principles and the Roundtable methodology. These women started to conduct their own Roundtables and they too were flourishing. God was blessing them.

God was setting up divine appointments that would help provide insight in addition to unleashing the power of collaboration.

Bernie Torrence met a man by the name of Clayt Sonmore in St. Louis, Missouri, in 1992. Clayt was like a Kingdom scribe and documented the amazing move of God he had witnessed.

Clayt was the person who put a deep calling into Bernie's life to write down everything that happened the way that it happened. Clayt was one of those transitional leaders that God always uses when He is moving from one place to another.

At this same time, John met a leader by the name of Dennis Peacocke who had an organization called Strategic Christian Services. John and Dennis had the same view of the Kingdom. John was asked to serve on Dennis's board. Dennis had formed a school known as the International School of Biblical Economics. It was based in Santa Rosa, California.

Both John and Dennis were aware that God was about to converge many streams of the Kingdom into a powerful organism… on earth as it is in heaven.

These relationships would become extremely important as God knew that John was about to once again face a major challenge which would bring much change.

In 1992, at IFCB's 3rd annual conference it became apparent that the vision and direction that God had given John was about to be challenged.

Unbeknownst to John, there had already been a lot of behind-the-scenes talk that had taken place. The issues that were presented at that meeting had already been pretty much decided prior to the meeting. Passing them was merely a formality.

The issues that were set forth and passed were:

1. IFCB would not promote the Kingdom of God message. Instead, they would remain evangelically focused.
2. IFCB was for men only — women's Roundtables would not be recognized.
3. IFCB would train businessmen on how to minister rather than how to impact the business arena with practical values and principles.

Once again, John found himself in familiar territory. The vision that God had birthed in John was not the vision that this organization would honor.

John had learned that these men met with various Roundtable leaders, informing them that John was no longer in charge and that they would now learn to conduct the ministry the right way. The writing was on the wall.

John's spirit was heavy, as what God had birthed in John was non-negotiable. Upon his return to Ohio, John formally resigned his position.

As these events were unfolding, Bernie Torrence had just finished reading a book written by Clayt Sonmore called *Beyond Pentecost* that had just recently been published.

This book discussed the outpouring of the Holy Spirit in 1953 and the birthing of a new organization. In 1953, God had placed a mantle on a group of "nobodies" and because of three things that mantle had been removed:

- Building a personal kingdom
- Over organization
- Not allowing everyone to participate in the ministry

Many big-name ministries in the United States were falling. God had warned them not to set up their own kingdoms. This warning was left unheeded.

One ministry after the next crumbled to the ground as they became exposed either for the private sin in lives of the ministers or within the ministries themselves. Christianity was taking hit after hit as corruption in major ministries were revealed.

As John and Bernie watched these ministries crumble to the ground, it became very apparent to them that it was no accident that Bernie had discovered that book.

People had been praying across the world for a birthing that would restore the move of God that began in 1953.

The time had come for John to establish a new organization that would focus on the vision and direction that God had given to him. This was to be an organization not plagued by former things. It would be created to usher in God's new mandate of His Kingdom and to propagate throughout the world.

The International Network of Christian's in Business was founded on June 26th, 1992, by John Schrock, Bernie Torrence and Jerry Anderson.

Although Jerry was initially involved at the foundation of this organization, God would call Jerry back into business less than a year later.

The term "network" in their name "International Network of Christian's in Business" was chosen prior to the formation of the internet. Initially it met with mixed reviews. However, in time, the concept of "network" became so easy to understand as the internet rolled out. Nearly overnight, everyone was experiencing what it was to be connected together.

The following guidelines were established for INCB:

1. It cost to belong to this organization, it did not pay. This showed the position of the heart's of the men and women that participated. Each member's expenses would be paid by the individual, not by the ministry, including John's.

2. To ensure that no one set up a kingdom of their own, this ministry would be "faceless."

3. This ministry was both for men and women — everyone was welcome to join.

4. INCB was to serve as a training platform.

This organization's mission was to establish God's

Kingdom operating system on earth through teaching of values and principles found in the book of Proverbs. The principles were written in a format with only one principle discussed per week. The categories are broken down by:

Self Government
Motives, Morality, Attitude, Emotions, Proper Thinking, Parameters, Patience, Restraint, Temper, Forgiveness

Productivity
Ambition, Dependability, Goals, Hard Work, Productivity, Common Sense, Direction, Effective Planning, Facts, Responsibility

Management
Ownership, Honesty, Humility, Generosity, Trust in God, Saving, Sowing, Debt, Co-Signing, Prosperity

Leadership
Pressure, Understanding People, Developing People, Listening, Inspiration, Conflict, Confrontation, Chastisement/Correction, Criticism, Judgment

Each "value" category contained ten individual life-giving principles. This leads to a 40-week commitment for each person in attendance. The attendees were not to exceed eight people per Roundtable group. Knowing that business people had very limited time, this ensured that a Roundtable meeting would not exceed one hour.

Jamie Roman from Ibague, Colombia, coined the phrase "the altar of the Roundtable." Jamie saw the needs of business men and women were being reached at this "altar" rather than the church. Normally because of their higher standing, many leaders had an inability to really express their needs at their church.

As business leaders discovered this organization, a request would be made by the sponsor for the INCB team to hold a seminar for all of those invited to attend. The seminars they held created a powerful event that became the catalyst and the Roundtables provided the process.

This organization grew through divine appointments. Regardless of where they went, God placed the right men in their path. If a flight was missed or if they agreed to drive a stranger to their destination, God was at work creating divine appointments. He was building their faith while creating a network of people that would become hugely instrumental in this organization's success.

INCB partnered with a major move of God taking place at this same time in Central America. This led to an incredible amount of fruit for INCB. God showed up in big ways and constantly gave them confirmation that He was with them.

At a meeting in Bucaramanga, Colombia, God moved so dramatically that 153 people gave their hearts to the Lord. It was at this time that a man approached Bernie saying, "La red, La red" (the net).

He went on to say that, "We have fished these waters for many years, but caught no fish" (meaning that they had taken the Gospel to the business community but had caught no fish).

He then said, "Today you have taught us to fish from the

other side of the boat. You have brought us a new net to use and that net is now full! These are BIG FISH."

John 21:11 NIV, *"So Simon Peter climbed back into the boat and dragged the net ashore. It was full of large fish, 153, but even with so many the net was not torn."*

God was at work and it appeared that God Himself was about to change the name of INCB. How appropriate that it would now be called La Red (The Net). John and his team yielded everything to God and allowed Him to be God and to use them as the vessels for His Divine purpose.

God taught them along the way as they were pioneers and forerunners. There was no formal training ground on which they could learn. They were getting "on the job" training. They had to learn the hard way that they could not rely on themselves or on their own talent. One such time in 1992 had put John, Bernie and Jaime's very lives in jeopardy.

God had given John a dream of three eggs in a basket. The team discussed this dream every day, asking if God had given any of them insight into the meaning.

They came to the conclusion that the eggs represented the three South American countries, Argentina, Chile and Peru that they were entering. They believed that if they pressed on hard enough that the eggs would hatch. God was opening up these countries and they were ready for the teachings La Red was bringing to them.

As they encountered obstacles along the way, they

interpreted it as they needed to push through the obstacles in their path. They gathered up the physical strength necessary to endure these obstacles. They were confident that the resistance they were facing was due to the breakthrough they would be encountering.

During their travels within these three countries, they encountered every type of obstacle imaginable. Bombings had become a normal occurrence in Bogota, where the team was flying from. Peru, where they were traveling to was at war because of a group of rebels known as the Shining Path. All travel was suspended for non-Latin Americans. The team literally had to find a way out of this nightmare and fast.

Flights were canceled, airlines were not honoring previously booked flights and there was chaos all around them. The situation had grown dire and immediate.

The team agreed that John needed to be the first one to make his way out. John managed to get a flight on a standby basis. Bernie and Jaime remained to find their own solutions out of this nightmare.

After Jaime made his way home, his church was very concerned and considered no longer allowing him to be part of this ministry. In reference to the incredible amount of emotional and physical stress Jaime had endured. They said, "You sent an old man home to us."

After days of chaos and travel, as Bernie awoke out of a deep slumber on the airplane home, he suddenly saw the three eggs. God instantly revealed that they did not represent three countries, that they represented the three of them, John,

Bernie and Jaime.

The lessons learned from this trip were many. They learned to always ensure that they remain under the wings of God's protection. To never again force their way into situations which they have no control. They also learned never to assume that the doors in front of them were from God. From that day forward, they would wait and seek confirmation before proceeding.

In time, they established what they would refer to as the "Velvet Army", a team of committed intercessors that would cover them in prayer. These intercessors became such a valued part of the team that they were frequently consulted in the decision-making process.

God Himself filled every office of His five-fold ministry. He sent the right people at the right time to fill them. Pastor, evangelist, teacher, apostle and prophet. This structure created an exceptional operating system utilizing each person's gifting and calling from God. This ensured that this ministry remained well-balanced.

They had humble beginnings. As they persevered, God was busy behind the scenes putting everything in His perfect order.

The trials and tribulations they had faced in South America proceeded a meeting that was to be held in Panama. Panama was chosen as a central location for all of those traveling from other countries. They could feel that God was leading them, but they had no clear direction. Much prayer proceeded these meetings.

That evening as John was praying to close out the meeting,

many people had chosen to stay due to the strong presence of God in that place. Soon the room filled with spontaneous praise and worship through song. One by one, people were brought up front and prophesied over. The atmosphere was electric.

Suddenly, John had an open vision as Jesus Himself was walking through the room. The presence of God was felt so strongly that people fell to their knees, face down as they were incapable of standing in His presence. Jesus was not there to confirm anything, He was there looking at the hearts of the people in the room. This was a test of motives and missions. It was a Holy moment. A moment none of them would ever forget.

Everyone realized the seriousness of what God had called them to do. Everyone knew that these meetings were a divine appointment as they were being called to a divine assignment from God Himself.

John lived and walked with the supernatural power of God. My favorite stories are those found during his days with La Red. As the author of this book, I can assure you that John did not share these stories freely. I have spent a great deal of time and effort gathering these stories.

John never elevated himself by sharing the stories. He simply and humbly followed where God was leading him. He made himself available as a willing vessel for whatever purpose that God chose to use him for.

John's walk with God was relational and he counted on God to lead him at all times. One such time was when John was walking into a meeting. Suddenly the sidewalk in front of him turned to wet cement and the footprints of Jesus went before him!

The La Red team had been introduced to Mike Poulin in 1992 by Milo Miller. Milo had previously been one of the congregants from the little white church days. Milo was called to missions in Mexico where he first met Mike Poulin. Mike was about to learn firsthand of John's unconventional style and his complete lack of decorum.

Mike had set up a meeting for John and the team in Allende, Mexico. Mike had spent a great deal of time gathering this group of people that missionaries had tried to influence for a lifetime and could never see or approach.

Major effort was put into preparing a world-class seminar for this group of hard-to-reach men.

The banquet room was filled as people gathered to hear the wisdom of God from this team of gringos.

As the meeting began and John was introduced to speak, John said to the team, "You know, the Lord is not here. We should quit right now." John knew their efforts would be futile without the presence of God going before them and working in the hearts of the attendees. In an unprecedented move, John shut down the meeting.

The team packed up, apologized and walked away with their tails between their legs.

Later, Mike told the team that they had impacted more leaders with this moment of humility than their seminar ever would have.

The year 1999 was very special in the development of La

Red. The La Red team was working very closely with Dennis Peacocke and his organization Strategic Christian Services (SCS). Both organizations could clearly see the move of God on the earth and how systems were changing.

At one of the SCS conventions, a guest speaker shared regarding his thoughts on Y2K. The professional leaders that were in attendance were totally caught off guard with this phenomena. The fear was that all computers would crash at midnight on New Year's Eve 1999 and render the world powerless. The entire spirit of the convention changed because the people could easily see how this computer phenomena could affect their organizations and their futures.

SCS was on the cutting edge. A number of symposiums were planned to prepare people for the upcoming fall of international computers in the year 2000.

John and Bernie were in attendance at one of the SCS meetings that took place in Colorado. The meeting was held in a castle owned by the Navigator Ministry. What took place at the closing session would not soon be forgotten by those in attendance.

One by one, the leaders gave their strategic plan and what their preparation and contingencies were as everyone was waiting for the world-wide meltdown.

When it got to John, he stood up and said, "You know, I cannot believe that God would do something this big and not tell me about it!" He continued, "We are having more faith in the meltdown then we are in God." He then sat down and people began laughing and thinking about what he had just said.

Of course Y2K proved to be nothing but a blip on God's timeline. However, there was something very special that happened in the year 2000 as La Red was being prepared to touch other nations.

John and Bernie were invited to an international strategy meeting in Davos, Switzerland, where various business organizations were unifying. It was hosted by Jurg Opprecht and a new organization called Business and Professional Network.

It was there that a prophetic image was given by Siegfried Burkholz. He said that the old world was based upon two axes. Nations that were rich and poor were on one axis and nations that were east and west were on the other axis.

He prophetically stated that the new world of this millennium would be fast and slow on one axis and young and old on the other axis.

He continued that it would no longer be rich ruling the poor and democracy versus communism. Instead it would be a flat society that offered equality and access for all.

In the coming years they saw a great equalization involving laptop computers, cell phones, internet broadband and smart phone devices. God had brought this massive change not by Y2K failure, but by innovation and invention. This has proven to be an accurate picture of the word of God in our world today.

La Red grew through a never-ending series of divine appointments set up for them by God Himself. God led them through supernatural experiences, prophetic words, dreams, visions and divine appointments the same way He continues to lead them today.

In 2004, at a weekly leadership and planning meeting between Bernie, Jerry and John, John walked into the room and resigned his position as International President of La Red. John said he would continue to spend time writing and encouraging the team, but he felt the travel schedule was becoming more than he was physically able to maintain.

That was the extent of the meeting that day. In the typical John Schrock fashion, he said what he had to say, then got up and left the room. Bernie and Jerry looked at each other as both were left pretty much speechless. They were not sure what to make of it. Was John serious? Shouldn't they have discussed the future of La Red? Who was going to assume John's position? What in the world had John just done?

The following week Bernie and Jerry met on the same day, time and at the same venue. When John did not show up for this meeting they realized that John was, in fact, serious regarding stepping down. John's resignation meant that the leadership would fall on either Jerry or Bernie, and Bernie was adamant that he was a Captain not a President. Jerry was convinced that he would be a horrible President. He agreed to take the position just to show Bernie that it was, in fact, Bernie that was the right man for the job.

Jerry Anderson assumed the position as International President. Jerry was, in fact, the right man for the job, as Bernie had known all along. As prayer was given for Jerry that day, not only did Jerry receive the title of International President, he received a double portion of the mantle that God had placed on John. The mantle stays with the mission! Jerry was walking in divine favor!

Under Jerry's leadership La Red has grown in unprecedented proportions. Today La Red is in over 100 countries.

After John's retirement, he said, "La Red is accelerating because this message was not just for me, it is for the world."

After the death of my dad in 2011, I wanted to ensure that my son and nephew knew who their grandpa was. What better format to educate them in than by us holding a weekly Roundtable meeting.

It was during this time that I realized another value of La Red and the Roundtable process that I had not previously understood.

As my family went through each principle. I realized how this format was teaching our young men principles and values in life. Now, that doesn't seem surprising I'm sure. But here's the thing, they were learning the principles when that particular principle was not a current issue in their lives. It meant that this made them much more receptive to receive the message. This was a proactive approach not a reactive approach.

As a parent, this gave me great comfort. I knew that they now had full knowledge of God's principles. They were learning things that may not have become an issue in their lives until years down the road. As a parent, I could rest assured that they were armed with God's value system and truth that would lead to success in their lives.

For most of my life, I had viewed La Red as strictly a business training platform. I thought La Red was all fine and good, but I already knew the principles. It was no big deal to me. Introducing it to my family showed me another invaluable purpose. What I had known until this point was only the beginning of the value that the La Red principles brought to the table.

The amazing thing about the principles was that it did not matter what ministry mountain you are called to. Be it the mountain of religion, family, education, government, media, arts and entertainment or business. God's principles will transform any and every environment through the transformation of the hearts and minds of people.

As I was researching the information for this book, I was reintroduced to a book that John wrote in 1993, *Thy Kingdom Came*. This book was written right after the formation of La Red. I read this book when it first came out and it was an easy enough read or so I had thought. The depth of the message somehow had managed to elude me the first time I had read it.

Nearly 25 years later as I once again read this book, I realize that it is perhaps one of the most relevant books I've ever read regarding the times we are living in today. It is complete with God's solution for the world's problems that we are facing today. John does not just spell out the problems, he teaches the solution.

For the first time, as I have had to study this ministry for the purposes of this book, I get it. I see the big picture and I am blown away as to what it is that I see. Could it actually be this simple? I believe it could, in fact, be this simple. We make it complicated.

I can also see why many churches may have a problem with the message. I realize what is at stake. However, I propose that the churches that embrace this message and teach it will, in fact, turn out to be the most relevant churches in the future because they will hold the solutions. Just as the vision that God gave to John says, "The world will come to Christians for answers."

Today, I have a completely different view of La Red than I did in the past. As I read my father's book I realize La Red is something far greater than what I had the slightest clue regarding.

Excerpts from the book, *Thy Kingdom Came*, written by John E. Schrock.

"Principles of Value"

Jesus said (in Matthew 5:13), "You are the salt of the earth. But if the salt loses its saltiness how can it be made salty again? It is no longer good for anything, except to be thrown out and trampled by men." (NIV)

The thought is that if the people of God lose God and His values, they will be rejected and discarded by government and people in general, because anything that has value will be used, preserved and protected. If Christianity has no value to offer, such as quality leaders with creative, solution-oriented ideas, they will not have any influence on a society.

God's laws and principles were meant to be practical and usable. They were to influence and be solutions. However, we have taken God and His word to church, and have left societies to find their own way. Christianity is now branded as just one of the many religions. We have made heaven our goal and rapture as a way out of our situation.

Our way of thinking is now rejected and put under the feet of men, as Jesus said it would be. Jesus was saying, "Follow my ways and I will make you a valuable resource; and you won't be rejected." Good apples are not thrown away; they are used.

All through the Bible, we can find the principles of value. God always resolved problems by finding men and women of valor. For every need, He found a man, and in this man, He placed a vision of "the right way to rule" which became solutions. Men and women of valor (value) are respected and used. They offer good advice and solutions.

This is also true as the light of the world. Who would reject light (insight that brings solution) when things seem hopeless? One of our problems is that our light and salt are perceived as religious and impractical. We might ask ourselves the question: Who is responsible for this perception and how can it be changed?

"The Challenge"

Things can and will change, because it is in God's plan. It is all a part of His master plan. We can change our personal outcome, but not God's eternal plan. We can only choose to participate in His plan or reject it.

You and I were created in God's image. We are like God in that we can reason, imagine, create and make choices. This gives us many options.

God created life with a purpose and a goal in mind. He knew the outcome before He started. He is in control of the earth's destiny. His plan and purposes will be fulfilled.

We (mankind) are the only part of His creation that has the ability to choose, to change and to create.

Birds have built their nests the same way for thousands of years — no change in styles, no trends to follow and without creative competition or even imagination.

All living things are created after their own kind. Man, however, can take that which God has made and by cross-breeding, create hybrids. However, when left alone, it will revert to its own kind.

God has created us in His likeness and image. It was a dangerous thing to do. We have the ability to forsake God and His ways. We can choose to do our own thing, our own way. We have the power to form our own rules and ethics. We can even denounce and rebel against God.

God created His own potential competition. However, He also created a system of laws (natural and spiritual) that would protect His plan and end those who would rebel against it.

He knows that in the end His laws will accomplish what they were designed to do.

So, in His kingdom He has given us an opportunity to live and enjoy living. He made us like unto Himself. He has feelings. He can be sad. He can be glad. He can be hurt. He is jealous over us as His children. He is loving and caring, but also just. He is fair, honest and righteous. He is a good Father and God.

He has created us with the same feelings and emotions. He has given us opportunity to be like Him. He enjoys us as we can enjoy each other. Life was not meant to be difficult because of our own choices. We may have done things out of ignorance, but the laws of God's creation don't know the difference. Gravity will not argue with you. You can't explain that you didn't understand it. Gravity just does what it was created to do.

Similarly, it is important to learn about God and His laws. Knowing the truth will make us free, because we respect and work within the framework of God's fixed laws.

We can get away from God's planned life by the use of our creative gift of choice that God has given us. We can decide to do things our way. We can follow our imagination and lift ourselves up, make our own rules and try to re-invent life. We may think we know best, "We can do it our way." It will turn out to be a learning experience, to say the very least. God's principles will break us; we cannot break them, they are fixed.

Sooner or later, we will discover that our ways will become hard and difficult. The point is we will not change God's plan and destiny. It will happen just the way He planned it. His kingdom will come in its fullness shortly, because the world is going to become so messed up under the rule of humanistic thinking that it will collapse. We will go bankrupt. Taxes will become unbearable. Special interest groups will fragment our societies to the point that societies will become unmanageable. Civil wars will break out. There will be hell on earth until we learn and turn to the principles of God's kingdom.

We can choose to participate or not to participate. If we do participate, we will rule with Him and enjoy life the way He designed it. If we don't participate, we will be ruled by those who do.

There are no other options. God's code of ethics will be the rule. His standard of righteousness will become the standard of law and justice throughout the world.

I can't change it. You can't change it. America can't change it. The United Nations can't change it. And no religious groups can stop it. Just as Jesus came in His appointed time to bring us the kingdom, so there is an appointed time for its fullness to come. Some will hate it and be destroyed, but no one will change the plan. The plan is fixed. Others will love it and participate. They will be blessed and have a great time. They will watch the unrighteousness rule fail and collapse, and will be there to restructure it under the laws of God's kingdom.

The time will come when most of us will have to eat and live on a diet of unrighteousness until we are sick and tired of being sick and tired. We will then participate and call for God's kingdom of righteousness to come to earth to deliver us from the judgment of unrighteousness.

Even so, my Lord and King, we welcome Thy kingdom to come and Thy will be done on earth, as it is in heaven.

If you would like to purchase a copy of this book please contact:
La Red Foundation Headquarters
5555 County Road 203, Millersburg, Ohio 44654
Phone: 330-763-2121 // E-mail: info@lared.org

A radio announcer from San Francisco somehow obtained a copy of this book. He stated on air, "This will be one of the greatest Kingdom books ever written." He then proceeded to read and record the book in its entirety.

The book *Thy Kingdom Came* was so far ahead of its time and so strongly prophetic, they knew that they would blow most people who were reading it out of the water. They divided the book into several booklets and removed a lot of the doctrines. All of the teachings are as relevant, if not more so today, than when they were first published in 1993.

If you grasp the message, you will never again look at our current events in the context of these people just need to be saved. Yes, they do need to be saved, however, what John is teaching is a Kingdom operating system that works for all of mankind. Pick a mountain and this system will work.

I would also propose to you that as people go through the 40-week Roundtable process that these truths create fertile ground for the Holy Spirit to work in their hearts.

> *"The principles will revolutionize the world. The world is meant to be full of righteousness. Jesus said, the Kingdom of God is righteousness, peace and joy. Any nation that practices righteousness, real righteousness, no lying, no cheating, no stealing, they will experience peace and joy. Those are Jesus's own words."*
>
> —John E. Schrock
>
> *"I've been thinking about this divine appointment that we all had, not realizing the kingdom connection that Pastor David always talks about. It now seems that this was much bigger than any of us could have imagined. I now see a Caleb passing the baton to our group to take the next mountain."*
>
> —John E. Schrock

Today there are several branches from the La Red tree that have been established. All are based upon the original 40 principles. In the world that we live in today with the separation of church and state, the legalities of these teachings must be in alignment with the venue (mountain) in which they are taught. Although the principles are the same, several programs do not contain the Bible scripture verses themselves upon which these principles were founded.

Global Entrepreneur's Institute — GEI:
Online course using the 40 original La Red principles

Global Priority Solutions — gps:
45 personal development values

Character Development for Schools:
Non-profit character and leadership

Foundation for Achievement:
40 original La Red Principles written by John Schrock

There were, and are, so many men and women that are noteworthy throughout the La Red story. I have specifically focused on John, Bernie and Jerry as in my opinion they all hold the founder title in some regard.

It is impossible to give credit to every person that spoke into this organization, gave selflessly of their time, energy, money and worked tirelessly on this mission and continue to do so today. I also know that none of them including John, Bernie and Jerry have done this for fame or to establish their own kingdoms. They have been part of the incorruptible seed that was planted by God Himself.

The HPD platform that John had built (restaurant, hotel and fitness center) became the place where those traveling for trainings and meetings for La Red would meet and hang their hats for the night.

Today, although there is no longer a restaurant, this same facility, under Jerry's ownership, serves the same purpose on a much grander scale. Today they house and train people from all over the world. I find it fascinating that just as the mantle for La Red was passed on to Jerry, it appears the same may in fact be true for the facilities that these meetings were held in. Coincidence or God's plan? I don't know, but I certainly find it fascinating.

Was John's entrepreneurial life a success? I think the answer should be quite obvious. It no longer seems significant does it? You cannot remove John's business success from his ministry success. They are one and the same. John's success in business financially fed the ministries that he founded. They are not separate of each other. John's legacy was in building the Kingdom of God. No earthly success compares! Plain and simple!

The absolute irony of the La Red story is that it completely mimicked John's belief system as a child that he gained through that Bible storybook that his mother got him. God spoke to a man and in this case that man was John. God called that man to solve a problem. God raised the standard; a Kingdom operating system of values and principles and used John to bring life, truth and restoration to a situation; a world in chaos and turmoil. The God of those Bible stories is alive and well and still at work in the situations of the world today.

Hebrews 13:8 KJV, *"Jesus Christ the same yesterday, and to day, and for ever."*

"Life turns out to be, what you really believe."
—John E. Schrock

CHAPTER SEVEN

John's Foundational Lessons for Living a Life of Abundance

Overcoming Fear

2 Timothy 1:7 NKJV, *"For God has not given us the spirit of fear, but of power and of love and of a sound mind."*

When John was 15 years of age, he was entrusted with plowing the fields at his family farm.

Plowing fields for the Amish meant using horses, not modern-day farm equipment. This was not a one-day job.

The electric company had gained permission to put up a huge tower to run their power lines on Eli and Barbara's land. This tower stood 116' tall and was located in the same area as the field John was plowing.

Prior to the electric company adding the power lines to the tower, while resting the horses, John set his sights on climbing the tower and reaching the top. Each day he would make more and more progress until one day he made it to the top of the tower and sat down to take a look around.

As he was sitting there, he started to wonder what it would be like to actually stand on top of the tower instead of sitting. He had already reached his goal of climbing to the top of the tower perhaps he should set the next goal of standing on it.

John pondered this idea for a while and soon realized that what was keeping him from doing so — fear. So, John devised a plan on how he might be able to overcome his fear.

He set up the exact same scenario on the ground using bricks on each end to support the boards on top. In the evening, when all the chores were finished and he had time on his hand, he practiced walking this board. Night after night, John walked that board over and over and over again trying to visualize himself as doing so at the top of the tower.

Finally, one day, he believed he was now mentally prepared to stand at the top of that tower.

John climbed the tower and sat there for a while as he had done many times before. This time he visualized himself as actually being on the ground like he had been while he was practicing.

He reminded himself that the only thing keeping him from accomplishing this goal was fear. When he had the visual in his mind of being on the ground, to the point that he could believe it, he stood up. He did it — he was standing on a beam at the top of that tower with his hands in the air 116' feet from the ground. (Aren't you glad he wasn't your son?)

John shared that story hundreds of times with thousands of people. He said if you want to overcome fear, simply do what it is that you fear. Devise a plan if necessary, practice, but ultimately, you just have to push yourself to do the exact thing you fear.

The Narrow Way: Proper Thinking

This teaching is based from the scripture found in Matthew 7:14 KJV, *"Because strait is the gate, and narrow is the way, which leadeth unto life, and few there be that find it."*

One day as John took a different route home from work in Canton, he saw a billboard that referenced Matthew 7:14.

On the billboard were two mountains. One mountain had a narrow road that led to the top of the mountain. At its peak was a rainbow, crowns and the word "heaven." The second mountain had a wide road to the top. On top of that mountain there was fire and the word "hell."

Upon returning to his home, John immediately looked up the scripture to get context. He discovered that nowhere in the scripture did it refer to heaven and hell. The passage was in reference to life here and now, although based upon your life choices in the end it could lead to heaven or hell. But that was not what Jesus was teaching in this scripture.

That Sunday at church, John taught on this verse and he used the example of the children of Israel's exodus out of Egypt.

I'm sure you know the story, but allow me to put this into

the context that John used while teaching on the narrow way.

The children of Israel had longed to be free from the slavery that they were living under. They prayed and pled with God for deliverance from living under Egypt's bondage and their rules.

Moses told them about a land flowing with milk and honey that God had for them. Their goal was two-fold: they were sick and tired of Pharaoh's strong arm and wanted to escape from his rule and also wanted the good life of milk and honey.

As they were led through Egypt and across the Red Sea, God told them that they needed to stop at the mountain because they needed some new teaching for the new life He was walking them into. God knew that they needed new teaching or upon entry into the land of milk and honey, they would recreate Egypt as that was all that they had known.

For years the children of Israel had blamed Pharaoh for their problems: "If it weren't for those Egyptians, we would be different." This was somewhat true, but not necessarily the whole truth.

In essence, God was saying, "Come to the mountain and I'll give you laws and rules of My kingdom, which you can use to govern yourselves. These laws will become your constitution by which you will judge and rule your people. As soon as you have established this constitution within you, I will take you into the land of milk and honey."

The sad part of this story is that out of all of the many thousands or maybe millions of Israelites that left for the milk and honey, only two of them ever got there to enjoy it.

The rest of the people only experienced the first part of the promise: they escaped from Egypt, but they never got to the land of milk and honey.

Even though they were free (no longer ruled by Pharaoh and the Egyptians) they would not submit to the rules that God had given them. They wanted to be free of all rules. They did not want Moses or anyone else to tell them what was right and wrong. They wanted to be free.

Yes, they were Israelites and God was with them, but God could not establish Himself in them. He could not get them to think, believe and act right. They doubted God, complained about His provision, and accused Him of misleading them in the wilderness.

They feared the giants and the high walls, doubting God's ability to conquer and to perform His miracles. In the past, they had blamed Pharaoh and the Egyptians for all of their problems, but now they had a problem within themselves. They did not want another set of rules. They wanted the milk and honey their way. They wanted no part of killing giants and climbing walls. They wanted the blessings of the land without conditions or responsibilities.

They were too scared to conquer the people of Canaan. They hated the wilderness. Some of them even wanted to return to Egypt.

In the end, God kept them in the wilderness for forty years. God had to allow an entire generation to die, because they could not change their thinking as they still possessed a slave mentality.

The correlation between this story and the scripture found in Matthew 7:14 *"Because strait is the gate, and narrow is the way, which leadeth unto life, and few there be that find it"* is that God had to keep them in the wilderness "the narrow way" to teach them, to retrain their minds on how to live a life that would produce milk and honey.

It's in the narrow way where we are taught and mentored by God. This is what Jesus was referring to when He taught the narrow way leads to life. It's the retraining of our mind to ensure we understand the values and principles we need to live by in order to be successful in life. Jesus was teaching us how to live successfully. Jesus was teaching that there is a way that gives you life that leads to vibrant life. He outlined that there is a way that leads to life and it is the "truth" about things. There is also a way that leads to destruction and that is the refusal to live by truth.

We all want milk and honey and God wants to give that to us, but you also have to fight giants in order to get to the milk and honey. Look for the truth, follow the truth and you will enjoy the milk and honey that God has for your life.

The Kernel of Corn: Environment

In this teaching John references a kernel (seed) of corn. A kernel of corn placed on a shelf will remain a kernel of corn. It has no multiplication in itself without the right environment. It will always stay a kernel of corn for as long as it is kept on that shelf.

But plant the kernel (seed) in the right environment and add moisture and that one seed will reproduce up to 600 kernels in just one ear of corn. It has to die for the kernel (grain) of corn in order to reproduce. It's ability to reproduce and multiply is all about the right environment.

The same is true for us. We were all born with the seed inside of us. In order to multiply we need the right environment. What creates the right environment? The right environment comes from the right belief system and the right teaching. With the right teaching and belief system, you can accomplish anything that you set your mind too.

> *"I see this as an example or a demonstration, an illustrated message. If we let the wrong principles and values that have been holding us back die and let the seeds of the right values and principles replace them and grow, you will live in a new place, a higher place!*
>
> *There is no limit to where this seed can take us, except us!"*
>
> —John E. Schrock

The Plumb-Line: Alignment–Character

The plumb-line teaching is in regard to the benefit of a life being in alignment with God's values and principles.

The plumb-line finds the center of gravity — when it

is plumb a person can build high. It is in reference to your foundation. If you are off as little as ¼" the higher you build the more vulnerable the building will be to collapsing.

Jesus said in Matthew 11:30 KJV, *"My yoke is easy, and my burden is light."* A one pound plumb-line in alignment weighs one pound. But if the plumb-line leans, as the builders build, it increases in weight. The further off a plumb-line gets the heavier the load carried. If your life is in true alignment, life gets easy.

> *"Everything else you can take your strength and make it stronger, but with character you have to identify your weaknesses and seal the cracks or the blessings will fall through the cracks."*
>
> —John E Schrock

Ruthless Faith

As a young Christian, John practiced what he referred to as "ruthless faith." Practicing ruthless faith is when you refuse to accept anything other than what the Bible has to say about a given situation.

One such time for John came when he challenged God's word in regards to healing.

On a Wednesday evening after church service, John drove his family to the local dairy for an ice cream cone. The dairy was the only place open in Berlin after 8pm on a weekday. It was a very busy little place and many of the local people gathered there often to catch up on the latest happenings in town.

As John was walking across the main road — in his normal hurried style — he missed seeing an oncoming car. The car struck John and he went flying about 15 feet into the air. This caused a big commotion in that small little town.

The onlookers ran to John's aid to see if he was okay. Slowly but surely, John got up — but there was no doubt he was in pain. No matter how insistent people were, John absolutely refused to go get checked out at the hospital. He insisted that he would be okay.

But John was far from okay. He had fractured his arm and had broken his wrist and was suffering with excruciating pain in his back and hip.

One of the reasons that John refused to go to the hospital was that he was fully aware that they would put his arm in a cast. John had a business to run and he knew that cast would keep him from being able to work for 3–4 months. That was just completely unacceptable. This is when he made the decision to challenge God's word.

The next morning, John literally crawled out of bed. He weathered the storm, but not without major physical challenges. Regardless of those challenges, regardless of everyone insisting that John needed to go to a doctor for help — John absolutely believed that God would heal him completely.

Two to three months down the road, an insurance agent visited John at the Gulf station. The insurance agent was there to compensate John for the accident and in return he needed John to sign a release form.

John said, "I'm not looking for anything." The agent replied, "Come on, this is common. I am here to offer you a settlement so we can close this matter." John insisted that a settlement was just not necessary.

The agent went on to inform John that he was authorized to give him up to $35,000. John said, "Absolutely not, I am going to be okay. I am trusting God to heal my back and my hip."

The agent said, as he shook his head, "I have never heard of anyone refusing a settlement. Most people actually want more than I offer."

Without accepting any type of compensation, John signed the insurance agents release form. He was trusting God for a miraculous healing.

At a Sunday evening service at the little white church, a guest speaker from another country was preaching. As this man was preaching, John felt what he described as warm water coming out of his back. Confused as to what was happening, John stood up and it suddenly dawned on him that God was healing his hip and his back.

John was completely and totally healed that evening. He challenged God's word and God's word proved true. Everyone around John had believed that he would struggle with this injury for the rest of his life. But John trusted God, and God was faithful.

John refused to accept payment for his injuries, even though he had every legal and moral right to accept compensation. But John knew that meant that he was partnering with the injuries by accepting payment for them and that it meant he was claiming the injuries as his own. He refused to do so. He refused to accept that identity. To John, it was as simple as why partner with the injuries instead of partnering with what God's word says.

For the record, there were times that John did consult a medical doctor for treatment. He was not foolish or unaware of the value the medical community brings to people's lives. This particular example highlighted John practicing ruthless faith and challenging God's word. God was faithful!

Matthew 8:6–13 NIV, *"Lord," he said, "my servant lies at home paralyzed, suffering terribly." Jesus said to him, "Shall I come and heal him?" The centurion replied, "Lord, I do not deserve to have you come under my roof. But just say the word, and my servant will be healed. For I myself am a man under authority, with soldiers under me. I tell this one, 'Go,' and he goes; and that one, 'Come,' and he comes. I say to my servant, 'Do this,' and he does it." When Jesus heard this, he was amazed and said to those following him, "Truly I tell you, I have not found anyone in Israel with such great faith. I say to you that many will come from the east and the west, and will take their places at the feast with Abraham, Isaac and Jacob in the kingdom of heaven. But the subjects of the kingdom will be thrown outside, into the darkness, where there will be weeping and gnashing of teeth." Then Jesus said to the centurion, "Go! Let it be done just as you believed it would." And his servant was healed at that moment.*

CHAPTER EIGHT

Family Life

By now you must realize that the demands on John's life were great. As I'm sure you can imagine, at least one area in John's life must have suffered from a lack of attention.

John was a good husband and father, but in my opinion his weakest area would be found in our family life.

Please remember this, I am the youngest of four children. I was born right at the time that the little white church was also born. These were, without doubt, the most radical days of John's Christian life.

Shortly after my birth, John had also just become a business owner for the first time. There is no question that the responsibilities in John's life had become great at the time of my birth.

Each of us children have a different view of our childhood. I've come to understand that our different views are also greatly influenced by our birth order.

Many times, I have thought how interesting it would be if each of us children wrote a book on his life. I am quite confident that they would all be very different from each other.

What I am sharing with you is based upon my memories and I do not speak on behalf of my brothers and sister, only myself.

During my childhood, John pastored the little white church and worked at least 60+ hours a week at his business. Add to this the time he spent counseling church members, advising others in business and in life, performing at various venues with his music team and you will easily understand that there would not have been much time left for his family.

Regardless if it was helping John by keeping the books at the Village Gulf station, attending church, special services, traveling for ministry or when practicing or performing with John, Marie was always by John's side. This meant that I was not missing just one parent, I was missing both.

For many in ministry back in those days, sacrificing one's family due to ministry obligations was considered okay as long as it was done for the greater good. (Although I have a feeling that many of the children of these families might not agree that it is okay.)

Although our time as a family was very limited, John had a major influence in our lives. Good Christian values and principles were instilled in each of us. We all had a strong understanding of right and wrong.

John did not teach these values and principles to us

children as much as he modeled them for us. Most of our teaching would be found at the same place as the other congregants — at the little white church.

At 5'9", John was larger than life to me. He had a big strong voice and when he spoke, he spoke with authority and certainty. He had big strong hands from all of his years of working on the farm. He was a man's man.

He was a man on the go and a man on a mission...and taking the time to play with his children was just not going to happen, particularly for a girl.

His drive and determination were both his best and his worst assets. He was always on his way to conquering the next thing.

We children were required to attend every church service. Church services back then were Sunday morning, Sunday evening and Wednesday evenings. We were also expected to be present for every special service.

You might think that as a child I would resent having to attend that many services; however, it was just the opposite. It was at the little white church where I was the happiest and would feel the safest. These people, although many were not blood relatives, certainly were my family.

They, too, were fighting the same battles in the community that we were. Maybe not quite as fiercely, but they certainly were very much outcasts also.

Growing up in the little white church with all the supernatural happenings, I developed a very strong belief system in the God of miracles and His supernatural ways. I had a very strong grid for God. It was here that I learned never to underestimate what can happen when God is at work in any given situation.

It was outside the doors of the little white church that felt like a bit of a war-zone to me. My saving grace and safety as a child truly would be found inside the doors of the little white church.

When I was about ten or eleven years old, I wrote in the front of my dad's Bible these words: "Hi Dad! Remember me? Your daughter Joy. Why don't you come home sometime?"

I knew the best chance that I had of my dad seeing a message from me was if I wrote it in his Bible. To this day those words bring me to tears. I remember exactly what I was feeling when I wrote them. I longed for a normal family life. I longed for a dad. I felt hurt and abandoned.

Most of my memories of my dad revolve around the island in our kitchen. It was here that you would find us gathered around, listening to John's many stories of things he encountered. He was quite a storyteller and we found him highly entertaining. I remember thinking that he was truly invincible. Even as a young child, I knew God's favor was on him and his life.

My dad loved to tell jokes. They almost became his trademark. Most of his jokes weren't all that funny and yet they were. His laughter was contagious to everyone listening. He certainly did have a quick wit but for some reason, in my opinion, his choice of jokes left a lot to be desired.

I have very few memories of us eating family meals

together and only twice did we go on a family vacation. My dad was not good at downtime. Most of the time when he was present, he wasn't present — his mind was elsewhere.

There was a revolving door at our house. I can't even begin to put a number to how many people would end up living with us. If people were down on their luck and needed a place to stay, our doors were always open. This also greatly affected our alone time together as a family.

Oftentimes, John would counsel the people from our church at our home. There were no offices at the little white church as is commonly found today in most churches. Our home was small and the walls were thin. I was privy to nearly all of his counseling sessions.

I learned exactly how he would advise people based upon what the issue(s) were that they were dealing with.

This exposed me to more than I should have been exposed to as a child. I remember many times my heart broke when I heard the details of people's lives. These people from the little white church were like my own family and these things that I was hearing greatly affected me.

Johnny's Gospel Team regularly held music practices at the little white church. Being the youngest and a bit of an annoyance to my older siblings, my parents would normally take me with them.

I have often told my parents that as a child I spent more time sleeping on the pews, under the pews and in the baby beds at church than I ever did sleeping in my own bed. I did not mean this as a funny recollection or something that I remembered fondly. I meant it as what in the world were you guys thinking?

Due to the many issues that John had to overcome in his own life, John was not big on sympathy and had no tolerance for any of us children to feel sorry for ourselves. This was the man that practiced ruthless faith while in excruciating pain. Chances were pretty good anything that we experienced would have been looked upon as pretty insignificant.

This led to us children coining the phrase, "Schrock it off." When those words were spoken, we all knew that it meant — "just get over it." We still use this term to this day.

Rarely did we get into trouble — or maybe I should say that we rarely got caught. But when mom would say, "Just wait until your dad gets home," we knew it was serious and we quickly changed our behavior. We all had a healthy fear of our dad.

We didn't have a whole lot of rules at our house. There wasn't a set bedtime or even a curfew when I was in my teenage years. I always used to think that it was just because he was too busy. Implementing those types of things would require consistency and him actually being at home to monitor our behavior. But I'm no longer certain that that was the case.

Today I believe it was more about his unwillingness to take away our choices in life. I believe that he felt it best to allow us to be free to make even the wrong choices. Perhaps he thought we would learn best if we were corrected by the consequences in our lives for those choices.

However, if he ever thought we were pushing things too far

or were truly in harm's way, he would never have hesitated to step in. I can remember several such occasions.

John had incredible insight into God's operating system and I believe he applied it to his own children.

He also knew what it was like to never have free will as a child. Perhaps he felt it important not to take it away from us. I'm not so sure that it was the right way to do it, but with all of his life experiences, I can understand how he might have come to that conclusion.

Berlin, Ohio, back in those days was a very small town. We knew every person that lived there. Most of the families had lived there for generations.

John, the son of a highly regarded Amish Bishop, had been excommunicated from both the Amish and Conservative Mennonite communities, lived in notoriety. This led to John becoming incredibly well-known in this little town and amongst the Amish and Conservative Mennonite communities throughout the state and even surrounding states.

John became the target for many people that hoped to elevate themselves by winning a Biblical debate against him.

We could be anywhere; at a festival, at a family reunion or even at the Village Gulf station and in no time another battle would be underway. It was almost like watching a gun fight, but instead of guns, it was with Bible scripture.

Regardless of where you might have found John or any of us on any given day, you'd also find a group of people whispering amongst themselves.

We were raised with our first language being Pennsylvania

Dutch. Although we may not have been dressed Amish we certainly could understand the things these people were saying. None of it was nice and certainly not worthy of repeating.

Watching all of this fighting due to different religious beliefs and different interpretation of Bible scripture created a major disdain and dislike inside of me. Religion and religious people were so contrary.

I could not reconcile in my head or heart how people that considered themselves to be Christians could have said such hateful things about my dad, our family and our church. Early in life, I had to learn how to navigate myself as an outcast from the community. I was an outcast simply because I was John Schrock's child.

My struggles in life more than likely could have been avoided or at least eased with a little more parental guidance and consistency. However, my parents were so busy fighting their own battles to survive that they were completely unaware that these battles would also have an effect on me.

I am very relationship based. I didn't really have a relationship with my dad as a child. I was different from my brothers and sister. He did not stop to evaluate his children's differences in personalities. What worked with my siblings would not work with me. I viewed my dad as hit and run and I did not respond well to that. Instead, I rebelled against it.

My whole life I had been judged simply for being John Schrock's child and I fought with everything I had for my own identity.

In my mid-teenage years, when John belonged to that first Christian business men's organization, I had reached a boiling point. That organization had an annual conference that fell every year over Thanksgiving and lasted throughout the weekend.

I absolutely could not comprehend that my parents would abandon us over Thanksgiving. My interpretation of that was what kind of parents would do that? What kind of organization would require that? What kind of God would honor that?

Every other family in our community celebrated the holiday together. Thanksgiving is a big deal. Instead, my brothers and I were left to fend for ourselves. That was when I went from feeling hurt and abandoned to feeling angry.

As the little white church grew into the "grown up church," the politics of church entered the scene. Suddenly there wasn't just one pastor, there were several, including an entire staff of people to manage. To me, this wasn't church — this was a business.

By that time, combining all of my life experiences, I'm sure you can understand that all I wanted was to escape all of this craziness. I couldn't wait to move out and get away from it all.

Nothing would ever replace the little white church that I had so dearly loved. Those days were gone and so was I.

It would be nearly 30 years before I would willingly — without a great deal of pressure — step foot into a church again.

CHAPTER NINE

The Prophet's Daughter

Separating the Acts of Man from the Acts of God

God was at work for many years setting up all of the pieces that would be necessary to lead me into truth and freedom. In order for you to grasp the magnitude of what God has taken me through, I need to share a bit of my own life story prior to sharing the journey that God took me on as I was writing this book.

As you know, my relationship with my dad was very complex. What you do not yet know is that I spent nearly 20 years of my life working by his side in business. We did not have a father/daughter relationship as much as we had a business partner relationship.

That business partnership relationship would come crashing down on Thanksgiving Day in 2001.

Yes, once again, another painful event in my life regarding my dad would take place on Thanksgiving Day. I will not get into the specifics of the event itself as it truly would require yet another book. That event was 40 years in the making. What I will say is that was the day that my blinders were removed by God. That was the day that I saw myself as a little girl who spent her entire life striving to earn the unconditional love of her father.

I was not mad at my dad, I was mad at myself.

That day I suffered a blow so great that I had a moment of truth with God. What happened that day would either leave me bitter or better. I chose the latter — to be better.

That was also the day that I learned that God was not to blame for my wounds. I learned that in order to see God in the proper light that I needed to separate the acts of man from the acts of God. It was that simple and yet profound!

This realization removed God from the equation of pain exactly the way that He should be. Once I saw God in the proper light, I wanted to have a relationship with Him. And it was through this relationship with Him that He led me exactly where I needed to go. This revelation freed me to pursue a relationship with Him. And pursue Him I did.

What that revelation did not provide was healing for the wounds I had sustained from the spirit of religion and religious people. God knew those still needed to be addressed.

God was Setting the Stage

After moving to California in 2007, leaving everything and everyone I had ever known, I found myself longing for a sense of community — a sense of community that just did not exist for me in California based upon my definition of community.

What I had not realized prior to the move is that for those 30 years, although I was no longer attending church, I was constantly surrounded by church.

In Ohio, I had always been surrounded by Christians. The vast majority of the people in the community that I lived in were Christian. Most of the people that I worked closely with were Christians. Even if a person was no longer involved or attending a church, they still had an ingrained knowledge of right and wrong. This meant that I was constantly surrounded by people that had the same value system that I had.

Now in California, particularly in the area where I landed, I found myself in a community where the reverse is true — those that identify themselves as Christian are the minority.

I would come to realize that it was the value system that I was surrounded by in Ohio that I missed. People's behaviors were predictable because they operated strongly with the same value system. The value system here in California varied significantly from person to person.

I knew the only chance I had of finding other people that had the same value system as myself would be to find a good church.

My other motivation to find a good church happened in

the middle of the night as I awoke out of a sound sleep. The TV was on and a documentary called "Frisbee: The Life and Death of a Hippie Preacher," a film by David Di Sabatino was playing on PBS. The interesting part of this is that there is no way that we would ever have had the TV turned to a PBS station. This in itself got my attention.

The next thing that got my attention was the actual scene on the television. I saw masses of people praising God and being baptized in the bay. As I continued to watch, I discovered that this move of God happened in California. I was floored. I longed to be part of that kind of movement. The freedom these people were experiencing was like that of the little white church and exactly what my heart longed for.

I was so restless at that time. Although my life was the best it had ever been in every way possible, I had this never-ending feeling of being incomplete. I had felt that way since my feet hit the ground in California.

Ironically enough, I had arrived in the Golden State on July 4th, 2007. I remember thinking how interesting it was that it just happened to be on Independence Day. I did not have a goal to arrive on that date, it literally just worked out that way. Perhaps this would be where I would find the freedom that I had been searching for my entire life.

My Jewish husband soon realized that if he did not help me find a church where I felt that I belonged, more than likely his reality would be us moving to Ohio. The thought of that was major motivation for him.

Through a series of events, my husband actually discovered

the church we would be calling home — the church that in time would become my new little white church.

One day, when out running errands, Alan returned with a business card. As I looked at the card, I was confused. This was a business card for a church called New Life Christian Center. He proceeded to inform me that he stopped by this church to see if they had counseling available. I was absolutely furious! I knew I didn't need counseling, I needed a community. I also knew that more than likely, Alan was hoping that counseling would solve the problem as the alternative would be for "us" to attend church.

It wasn't long after this that I decided it was time to put forth the effort to find a church that we could call home. I thought we might as well start our search by visiting New Life Christian Center. It never occurred to me that we would look no further. But that's exactly what happened.

We first visited New Life towards the end of 2010. We stayed pretty much under the radar. I purposely avoided building any close friendships with other attendees or anyone in a leadership position. I had even learned how to dodge the greeters at the door. Before I would allow myself to be known, I needed to know that I was in a safe place.

I did not want to know about their politics; I did not want to know the gossip; if there were cliques, I did not want to know that either.

Although we had visited several other churches in the years prior, I never felt compelled to return a second time. New Life was different, I could not stay away.

I was initially drawn to this church because of the freedom that I saw in the people as they worshiped. I hadn't seen that type of uninhibited worship since the little white church days. I remember standing there watching and longing to be free like they were.

I analyzed absolutely everything about this church.

Even though I had not attended church for a long period of time, I was fully aware that most churches no longer held services on Sunday evenings. New Life Church actually still had services on Sunday night. That was by far my favorite service, although attendees were few.

The informality of a Sunday night service allowed for the Holy Spirit to flow freely and just like the little white church days, they followed the Holy Spirit's lead.

In this church I found a very strong sense of family, just like at the little white church. You could tell these people really liked and cared for each other.

Many people at New Life were transplants from other states. Many had very little family in California, if they had any at all. Just like the little white church, the people in this church became each other's family.

This church was located in an area where what they believed was not accepted from the community around them. This time it was not because of other religious views. This time it was because the majority of this community didn't even recognize that God exists. In many ways, the people in this church were rejects and outcasts from the rest of the community.

I intently watched Pastor Caleb's interactions with his family and I listened to any references he might have made from the pulpit regarding them. I analyzed the dynamics between Pastor Caleb and his wife, Rachel, and closely watched the behavior of his children.

Had I landed in a church where the pastor left his family behind with no regard, I would have never gone back to that church. To my surprise, what I discovered was a pastor that made his family as great of a priority as his congregation.

CHAPTER TEN

Open the Gates of Heaven

In mid-October 2011, during the time that we were attending New Life Church under the radar, I had been overcome by this overwhelming sense of death. I did not feel like my own life was in jeopardy, but that someone else's life was. It was all consuming and there was no question in my mind that the feeling was of death. This feeling did not come on slowly or increase over time. It just suddenly presented itself.

Throughout my life, I had always known that I had a strong spiritual sense regarding people, situations and coming events. Even throughout those 30 years that I refused to go to church, that spiritual sense was always present. I believed it gave me a competitive advantage in life and particularly in business. I often referred to it as my secret weapon. But this time it was different and far more powerful than anything I had ever experienced.

I had no clarity regarding whose life may be in jeopardy —

only that the feeling was of death.

At night, while lying in bed holding onto my husband, I'd say, "You promised me that you'd let me die first." We spoke openly and freely regarding neither of us wanting to spend a day on this earth without the other. We, of course, knew that we didn't really have any control over who dies first. It was our way of reminding the other of how much that we needed them.

The dread continued as night after night I cried myself to sleep. There was no way for me to have peace as that feeling stayed with me at all times.

I knew there was also no way for me to hide that something was wrong. I never shared what I was feeling with anyone other than my husband and children. I completely removed myself from any events or venues where I could potentially encounter people that I may know.

My dad's 80th birthday was quickly approaching. Bernie and my sister had planned a big celebration for this event.

I had just been in Ohio for five weeks in August through a portion of September for my daughter's wedding as well as to host a business event regarding a cause that I felt strongly called to be involved to promote.

During those five weeks I stayed at my parent's house. We had all spent a great deal of time together. It was truly the best time I had ever spent with my parents.

My husband's business is located in California, which required him to fly back and forth for the wedding and the business event we were hosting. He and my dad were having the time of their lives together. I had not anticipated them enjoying each other's company, but they certainly did. At that time my husband was extremely liberal and, of course, my dad was extremely conservative. They could not possibly have been on more opposite sides of the spectrum from each other.

As we were saying our goodbyes to my parents and making our way back to California, my dad hugged me and said, "I never thought you'd make it here for the entire five weeks." We both laughed because in the past that would have been impossible without major fights breaking out between us. I replied, "I've been trying to move home ever since I left."

I just could not comprehend having had a better time than during those five weeks. I knew his 80th birthday was a big deal, but to me, it would never come close to how great of a time that I had just had with them.

A party also meant the masses would be there. I knew it meant that I would not have had quality time with him. It would have been like my childhood all over again. I felt very satisfied with the time that I had just spent with him and my mom.

That feeling of death would not leave me and by mid-October it was completely overwhelming me as my spirit was continually on guard as I waited to see how this would play itself out. It was almost like I was holding my breath. I knew that I could not face anyone — particularly my dad.

Looking back, I find that incredibly interesting. After all, my dad was always my go-to person when I dealt with situations that I struggled to understand.

I had contemplated calling him to discuss this. However, I believed that I already knew what his response would be. He would tell me not give it any attention. He taught me that any attack from the enemy should never be given attention. (By the way, that is really good advice.) But the problem with that was that this did not feel like an attack from the enemy. To me this was a warning of what was to come.

The weight of the dread had grown so heavy that I could barely function. It took every ounce of strength I had to make it through the day. It was not uncommon to find me at any given time in my nightgown and robe.

I felt so guilty at the thought of not being there for my dad's birthday party. I knew he'd be excited about it and I did not want to disappoint him.

I must have checked flights no less than twenty times. Every time I contemplated booking a flight, I found myself physically incapable of doing so. It was like my whole being would become completely paralyzed.

As a last-ditch effort, I called Bernie for advice and his thoughts on how I should proceed regarding the party. In the typical Bernie fashion, it wasn't long before he had me laughing. It was decided that instead of attending, the West Coast Schrock clan would make a video to be shared at the party. We would also be present via Skype. The plan brought huge comfort to me as at least this situation was now handled.

Although my dad was a businessman throughout his life, he had either me or secretaries to handle anything related to technology. The previous Christmas I had bought him a laptop computer. Trying to teach him how to use it was no easy feat. He was determined to master it.

Around the last week of October, I was sitting at my desk in my home still dealing with what I would eventually refer to as depression. Although it was nearly lunchtime, I was still in my nightgown.

To my horror I receive a Skype notification that someone is calling. I checked to see who it was and to my relief, it was my dad. How he figured out how to place a Skype call was beyond me. In fact, it could have been truly viewed as a modern-day miracle.

Only because it was my dad, I answered. I was fascinated as to how he managed to place the call. He had the biggest grin on his face as he was so proud that he actually figured out how to use Skype. As I began talking to him, and with no response to my questions, I soon realized that his speakers must have been muted. Since I couldn't hear him and he couldn't hear me, communication would be impossible. Although he could not hear me, he certainly could see me. He must have thought it was hilarious that I would have the nerve to answer the Skype call while I was still in my nightgown.

It didn't really seem to matter to him that we couldn't hear each other. The only thing that seemed to matter was that he managed to place the Skype call without anyone's help. That infamous John Schrock grin remained on his face throughout this entire ordeal.

After a few minutes of trying to figure out what to do, I finally blew him a kiss and waved goodbye and clicked off of the call. I had no idea how much this would come to mean to me in the very near future.

On the evening of November 3rd, 2011, I received a phone call from my older brother, Jim. He informed me that my dad had just collapsed and they believed he may have suffered a stroke. They were currently en route via ambulance transferring him from our local hospital to Aultman Hospital in Canton, Ohio.

The minute I heard the news I knew that overwhelming feeling of death was in regard to the loss of my own father. I was completely and utterly in shock.

I told my brother Jim, "Keep him alive until I get there. Promise me you will keep him alive until I get there." He must have thought I was losing my mind. His response, "Well, I was hoping we'd keep him alive for a lot longer than that."

Oh man, what had I just said? No one outside of my immediate family had known what I had been experiencing. Fortunately, I was able to recover the conversation without exposing things by asking additional questions regarding dad's overall condition and symptoms.

I begged God throughout the night not to take my dad. When I say I begged God, I mean that I have never pleaded like that in my entire life for anything. I could not have slept more than five minutes at a time as the thought of living without my dad was too much for me to comprehend.

Unfortunately, my pleading did not change what I felt in my spirit. This felt very final, like it was non-negotiable with God. But now I needed to figure out how I would navigate my way through all of this when I got to Ohio.

The next morning, upon talking to my mom, she confirmed that my dad had a major stroke. Things were very serious. After the mishap with my brother, I was very careful regarding every word that I spoke.

Marie was not sure if it was necessary for us to fly home as of yet. Regardless of what she thought, I told her that we will be there late that evening.

That afternoon, my husband and I made our way home to Berlin, Ohio. I cried throughout the entire flight. I didn't care what anyone thought of me, as I was already in the grieving process. There was no way for me to stop the tears as the grief became all-consuming.

We arrived at the hospital around 11pm. The nurses allowed us to see him, but only for a few moments.

Looking down upon this man who was larger than life itself, hooked up to all of that equipment was nearly more than I could emotionally handle.

Although his eyes were closed and he could not speak, he was able to respond by squeezing my hand when I asked him to do so.

God, in His divine mercy, knew that there were many things that I needed to say to my dad prior to Him taking him home. Having the opportunity to do so was nothing short of a beautiful act by a kind, compassionate and loving Father. What a blessing!

There were people coming by to visit him non-stop. I remember feeling disturbed regarding all of the people who came to visit. You may think that I would have felt comforted. Instead I just wanted them to leave. We had shared him with the rest of the world for our entire lives and now we were expected to do so at his death.

I knew my feelings were selfish but I honestly didn't care. They were my truest feelings. So many people had been coming and going that even the hospital staff started to ask the question, "Who is this man, John Schrock?"

I remember many times in those few days that we gathered around in a circle, holding hands with the many visitors, praying for him to be healed completely. We all believed in miracles, we had been witness to many. However, in my spirit I already knew that this was not going to end the way that we were wanting. My spirit still felt like God's answer was final. I remember that after a few days he no longer squeezed my hand when I asked him to do so. I knew that moment that we would soon have to face the inevitable.

I had watched every single thing that happened around me very closely. I had watched all of the events around me and around my dad at all times. I was trying to figure out why God had given me the warning of my dad's death. I didn't know what to do or how to handle it. I never told anyone about the dread the entire time we were there. Perhaps the prayers and faith of others would change God's mind. I prayed it would do just that.

After days of sleeping on reclining chairs, we finally convinced mom into going with us to our hotel to get at least one night of sleep.

Early the next morning, the phone rang. It was the hospital asking us to return and to contact the rest of the family members to do so as well.

My mom and I were the first to arrive. Shortly after our arrival, the doctor and training staff met with the two of us. They proceeded to share the results of their latest tests. They said there was no longer any brain activity and the only thing keeping dad alive were the machines. The time for us to make a decision had come.

My mom absolutely refused to let him go. She argued with the doctor and adamantly refused to accept what was being said. Finally, she said, "I can take care of him, I can feed him." She was literally pleading with the doctor for my dad's life.

I allowed this to go on for a few moments as I needed to know her thought process. I finally stepped in to talk to my mom. This was the hardest thing I've ever had to do in my life.

I knelt down by my mom's side and proceeded to share with her all the reasons why we needed to let him go. It was like I, myself, wasn't even speaking. I would never have been able to reason like that on my own, not through this overwhelming grief that I, too, was feeling. God Himself had to have intervened.

I didn't want to let him go any more than she did. But I knew without a doubt that God was calling him home. After reasoning through every possible scenario with her and reminding her of what his wishes would be if he could speak, she finally agreed.

On the afternoon of November 9th, the hospital made

arrangements to move him into a big, beautiful room located in their hospice section. By that time the word had spread and once again the people poured into the room.

The room was packed with family, ministry partners and lifelong friends. They were singing old hymns from the little white church days. They were ushering dad into heaven with song. How appropriate, considering my dad's lifelong love of music and those songs.

Once again, I wanted to scream and tell everyone to leave. But in my heart, I knew that this was exactly the way that dad would have chosen to go if he had a say in it.

I now paid even closer attention to the happenings in the room as my spirit literally felt as though it could jump out of my body.

After several hours, I vividly remember a nurse walking into the room, adjusting dad's pillow and opening a window. I remember watching intently and thinking how odd that was. The nurse then walked over to him and said, "OK John, it's OK to go now."

As the nurse exited the room, Kathy Torrence (Bernie's wife) immediately followed her. As Kathy got outside of the door, the nurse was nowhere to be found. She had simply vanished.

Upon Kathy reentering the room, Bernie began to read a prophetic word over my dad that had just been called in. This prophetic word was given by Dennis Peacocke, a highly regarded minister and personal friend of John's from Santa Rosa, California. As Bernie started to read the words, my dad took his last breath.

"God gives us pioneers in every generation. He gives us spiritual fathers in every generation, He gives us prophets in every generation. When they go home, we then realize who they are by the legacy they leave. Eternity, move over! One such man is coming. Those of us left behind say thank you, thank you, thank you John. Your work of prayer has now begun."

I had not fully comprehended that my dad had just taken his last breath. I was in shock over the word "prophet." Are you kidding me, my dad was a prophet? Why didn't I know he was a prophet?

Did everyone else know this but me? I did not know that prophets were still in existence in modern day. I had actually never even thought about it until just that moment.

There was so much commotion happening as dad took his last breath that no one else in my family even heard the words that Bernie had spoken. The room was now filled with inconsolable people.

That night, as I was trying to sleep, the events of the last several weeks were playing out in my mind.

My husband lay awake too. He was also struggling to get a grip on all the events including how I knew in my spirit that I was feeling death. All of this was inconceivable to him.

Because of the little white church days, I had insight regarding the supernatural workings of God, but my husband certainly did not. No less than ten times throughout that night, he would nudge me and say, "Am I married to the daughter of a prophet?"

As unfamiliar as that concept was to me, it wasn't really all that surprising that if prophets did still exist today that my dad would have been one of them. But it shook my husband to his core. I did not have the time or the mental capacity to deal with him or with any of it. I knew what the next several days were going to be like and I knew I needed to be prepared as best as I could to deal with all of it.

The calling hours were held at Berlin Christian Fellowship — the grown-up church. The viewings were numerous and long as there were well over a thousand people that made their way through to pay their last respects. There were so many stories shared as to how my dad had affected their lives. There was no possible way to get people through the line quickly.

There was also no way to deal with the grief that I was feeling. I had pretty much gone into shock. Now I was just going through the motions.

The funeral service was filled primarily with family, including a huge portion of my dad's relatives — most of them were still Amish. My dad's ministry partners, including some from other countries, and many of our lifelong friends from the little white church days were also in attendance. It was a beautiful service.

After the service we proceeded to a plot of land beside the church that dad donated to them many years prior. Thanks to the church, that land would now become the Schrock Family Cemetery.

Several days after the funeral, my husband and I made our way back to California. We were both still reeling from all of the events over the previous ten days. Life, as we had known it, would never again be the same again.

CHAPTER ELEVEN

Prophecy: The Good, the Bad, and the Ugly

After the death of my father, Thanksgiving and Christmas were just around the corner. I could not comprehend going through even the motions of those holidays. Perhaps if I threw all of my energies into them, I could find a sense of normalcy. But that did not happen.

It would not be long before I was facing a deep depression. I had no one to talk to regarding the events that had taken place prior to my dad's death. I had no way to reconcile any of it.

I feared telling people about it. I thought they might feel betrayed that I didn't tell them so they, too, could have emotionally prepared themselves. The other option was that they may think I was losing it. I was in completely unfamiliar territory and at a total loss as to what to do.

My husband was very supportive of all of the stages that I had gone through in the grieving process until the anger

stage began to overtake me. I do not handle things well when
dealing with issues that are outside of my control. I became
very argumentative and very intolerant of other people's
problems and particularly of mistakes that could have been
avoided. It was like there was a rage that was building up
inside of me.

My husband insisted that I get help to find my way
through all of this. Even though I knew he was right, I really
didn't want to. When I was finally sick and tired of being sick
and tired, I contacted Pastor Caleb and asked for a meeting.

I found it quite a coincidence that I was now reaching
out to the same church for counseling that my husband had
previously discovered when he was in search of counseling
for me. The difference being, this time I actually needed
counseling. I needed relief from the pain.

This was when I decided to it was time to become known
at my church. This was when my pain was so great that I no
longer cared about anything but finding relief for it.

The day of the meeting, Pastor Caleb was running a few
minutes late. I was waiting for him in his office. Upon arrival,
he had an armload full of DVDs and as I took a look at what
they were, I could not believe my eyes. It was *Frisbee: The
Life and Death of a Hippie Preacher.* Well, well, well... what a
coincidence.

This was just the beginning of the many coincidences that
I'd come to experience over the next several years.

For nearly a year after the death of my father, the tears
rolled down my face at every service. I remember thinking that

the people in the church were more than likely referring to me as the woman who always cries. The Holy Spirit was on me so strongly that I absolutely could not help the tears… nor did I want too. He was bringing me much needed comfort.

I could not have landed in a better church. Somehow Pastor Caleb understood me and that could not have been easy. At that time, I did not even understand myself. I had so many questions regarding the workings of God. Why had God given me that warning regarding my dad's death? Did I handle it correctly? And I had a thousand "whys" regarding my own life experiences. My entire world was shaken by my dad's death and everything that I thought that I knew was suddenly in question.

What Pastor Caleb understood was that I did not need more judgment. Coming from a community where we are judged by our works, my view of my relationship with God was never greater than that of my own actions. I measured everything by my Biblical understanding of right and wrong — you reap what you sow and uphold values and principles. These things required our effort and/or works and are all things that are immediately measurable.

It would be here, in California, where I would meet and encounter the God of love, the God of mercy and the God of grace. These are things that we cannot earn, things that are freely given and are completely without measure.

Pastor Caleb was right, that was exactly what I needed and that was a total game changer for me. I was encountering God's extravagant love for me on a daily basis. As the pain of the loss of my father subsided, I soon found myself having so much fun with God.

It would not be long before I was just as free in worship as the other people in our church, if not even more so. I could have cared less about what anyone thought of me.

Now I was no longer dealing with just what I referred to as coincidences, I started to have some incredible supernatural experiences.

One morning, I awoke out of a sound sleep to the sound of pouring rain. Our house was well insulated, being awakened by the sound of rain was indeed rare. The weather in California is very consistent and it is very difficult to differentiate one season from the next. However, the rainy season in the winter is the exception. Winter had become my favorite time of the year.

The rain that morning was the first of the season. Excited, I woke up my husband and said, "It's raining!" I knew he heard me because he mumbled something back regarding that he had no intention of getting up to enjoy it with me.

We had blinds on all of our windows, but they were partially opened and I could see the rain was coming down so hard that it was literally sheeting against the window.

I made my way downstairs to get a better view and to perhaps go out and enjoy it for a moment. I swung open the door to discover that there was not a single drop of rain anywhere and not a cloud in the sky. What in the world was going on? It took me a moment to get my bearings, and then I knew this was God's handiwork. I literally found myself laughing. I had absolutely no idea what it meant, but I certainly was enjoying it. In time, I would come to fully understand the significance of this supernatural sign.

I kept Pastor Caleb apprised of these types of happenings and met with him periodically when I would become a bit overwhelmed. These were the beginning days of the many signs and wonders that I would encounter throughout this journey. I was having so much fun with God. I was completely child-like and I was having the best time of my life!

God's love for me was so compelling that all I wanted was more. Sunday morning and Sunday evening services were no longer enough. This was when I searched out the surrounding areas for special services and conferences.

Soon, everywhere I went I became a "prophecy magnet." I could be in a meeting in the middle of nowhere with fifty other people and I'd be called out and given a prophetic word.

I loved being on this journey here in California, as no one really knew what was happening. My journey was completely my own. Unless you were in my inner circle you were not privy to the happenings in my life at that time. That was exactly the way I wanted it.

That was until I was at Bethel's Prophetic Conference in Redding, California, surrounded by a thousand or more of my best friends — complete with a television crew. That was when God Himself outed me with a prophetic word.

Had Shawn spoken any other prophetic word over me other than one that included my dad, it would never have gotten this much traction. More than likely, I would have been able to continue to stay under the radar. But with this word, there was nowhere to run and no place to hide.

Many people who heard Shawn's prophetic word were completely unaware where I was in my walk with God at that time. Some even still knew me as the rebel child, the black sheep, the prodigal. It had been many years since I had worn those labels.

Word spread quickly as the following day I felt compelled to send a voice-recording of the word to Bernie and Jerry. I did not realize how quickly it would travel. I also had many friends that were watching the conference on Bethel.TV. The following day, I received phone calls, emails and texts and it continued for quite some time. This was all before a video on YouTube was ever published. When the YouTube video hit Facebook for the first time in October of 2015, a whole new level of craziness happened. These were primarily complete strangers.

Depending on how a person approached me regarding the subject of this prophetic word, I could pretty much put them into one of four categories:

"The Cheerleaders"

The first category would be those people that were just completely undone by the prophetic word. People that celebrated it with me, people that were claiming the word as their own. These people were (and are) my cheerleaders. They are excited and grateful for God to have given such a beautiful word, a word that would also bring comfort to others who had lost family members. The majority of the people that contacted me fell into this category.

"The Wounded"

The second category would be of those people who had previously received a prophetic word that had not yet come to pass. They were very aware of the amount of warfare that oftentimes takes place after receiving a word from God. These people were cynical. Even if they didn't say it, I could feel their warnings of prepare yourself and don't get too excited.

"Why You"

The third category is "why you." Now this is a category that I can relate too. These are people that look at me and think, "Why would God give *you* a word?" To those people, I say trust me, you aren't asking anything that I myself haven't asked God many times. I feel completely unworthy of receiving such an amazing word. It's not that I am worthy — far from it actually. However, I believe there is a key. I believe the key is that I was in relentless pursuit of Him, I made myself fully available to Him and I completely yielded my entire life to Him. To me, that's truly what created all of this.

"The Haters"

Oh yes, there were haters — a whole group of them in fact. This group accused Shawn of having trolled my Facebook page and getting the words of knowledge part off of my social media. Was it there? Yes, it certainly was. Could Shawn have done that? Yes, he certainly could have. But they forget, that only covered the words of knowledge.

The other thing they were saying is that Shawn was speaking to the dead. Really? I must have missed that in the prophecy. If he had, we all know that would not have been good. I'm quite certain that had that been said, more than likely Bethel would have shut down the service at that very moment. It was never said, and never implied. Jesus said, "Write the book."

There is really no difference between the vision that God gave Shawn of my dad in heaven speaking to Jesus about me and the vision that my dad had when he, too, saw and listened in on a meeting in heaven.

These people were also calling Shawn a false prophet. I'm not sure how they could make that determination since it would remain to be seen if this prophetic word would come to pass.

There is no question that the things that were prophesied in regard to what I would experience in the process of writing the book have come to pass. That happened without me even realizing or having the understanding of what was happening. If I wrote a book on the entire "learning journey" that Shawn prophesied, it would take a minimum of five additional books to contain it all. There are at least 50 witnesses that can attest to the happenings throughout my journey.

The comments these people were directing at me were things like, "It's too late for you. You are going to hell." Really? You are my judge and jury? You must be reading a different Bible than the one I'm reading.

Considering my life story, I find all of this to be incredibly ironic. Think about it for a moment. Think about my dad's life. He had two entire religious groups of people telling him the same thing. They weren't just speaking those words over him, the attacks included his family.

This isn't my first rodeo with these types of people and accusations. I've learned a thing or two by being John Schrock's daughter.

What if my dad had listened to what people were saying instead of listening to God? The thought of that is absolutely chilling. Can you imagine him getting to heaven, facing God and God saying, "I called you and equipped you to solve a problem in the world. But you allowed the words and the fear of man to stop you. You didn't believe that when I called you and equipped you that I would protect you."

My dad had a choice. God gave him free will just as He'd given us all. I know from my own experiences with God that when He's at work, and when He calls you, you know it. Would you really want to be responsible for being the person whose words caused someone to stumble and not fulfill what God called them to? I certainly would not.

My dad also had amazing prophetic gifting. I could share many stories of the things that he prophesied over people that came to pass. I can also tell you stories of things he prophesied over people that did not come to pass.

What many people forget is that the receiver of the prophetic word also has a responsibility. The receiver has free will just as I did. I could have chosen not to write this book. I didn't have the extra time to write it. I could have discarded it by telling myself that I'm a business person, not an author.

I watched my dad's life very carefully. As you know, I had no problem going up against him when I believed that he was wrong. However, I watched him be judged unfairly many times and yet he kept right on going regardless of what his critics had to say. Thank God!

It was brutal having to stand back and watch my dad take those hits. I also partially blamed him because he continually put himself in the line of fire. He didn't have a problem with it, but I certainly did.

Watching those attacks on him was the number one reason that I did not ever want to be involved with anything regarding organized religion or religious people.

As I was now on my own secret journey with God, there were two reasons that I didn't want anyone to know.

The first was the judgments and attacks from other Christians that have a different theological belief. Think what you want, but this has been my experience in life. To prove how true this statement continues to be to this day, get on Facebook and follow any ministry and read the comments thread. Nothing has changed from what I experienced and watched throughout my life. If anything, the facelessness of the people on Facebook has done nothing but increase the level of attacks. If you are a non-believer searching for answers and you stumble onto one of those threads, can you imagine what they must think? Do you really think they are saying to themselves, "I want what those people have or I want to be just like them." To me, there isn't anything as ugly as Christians attacking other Christians.

That was the second reason I didn't want anyone to know. I didn't want any of the ugliness touching the most beautiful experience of my life. This was why I did not want to be seen or known. That was why, just like my dad during his Amish years, I kept my beliefs silent.

I had learned early in life that not being seen was where I had felt safest. I had mastered being hidden so well that it was very common for me to hear the words, "I didn't know John Schrock had another daughter."

Shawn's prophetic word had put me in the line of fire. It absolutely outed me. But through the journey over the last three years, I've learned that the only safety that I'll ever truly have can solely be found by trusting God and living in His perfect will for my life. As much as I wanted to continue to hide, that never was an option. I knew I had to write the book, as being disobedient to God was also never an option. God had cornered me and vulnerability had become my reality.

As I said, my whole life I've watched my dad take hits from religious groups. It was a difficult position trying to defend him since he was my dad. People could easily say that I had a bias. But I have no bias where Shawn Bolz is concerned. If anything, I could easily be upset with him for having outed me.

Can you imagine being Shawn Bolz and having that kind of gifting? Can you imagine the amount of faith in God that it requires for him to have the courage to walk out that gifting in his life? Ruthless faith!

Shawn is speaking prophetic words over people. These are things that have not yet happened. You may think that puts Shawn in a safe category as no one ever knows if these things come to pass or not. But you could not be more wrong.

If they do not come to pass, does that make Shawn a false prophet? Think about that for a moment. You absolutely cannot and will never know the answer to that question. There are many variables at play. Just like me, the receiver of the prophetic word also has a responsibility that requires effort.

First, it is each person's responsibility to judge the word. Second, it must be claimed. Third, it must be walked out. And fourth, in my opinion is the most difficult, timing. The timing must be right. Sounds easy? Trust me, it isn't.

Don't think for a moment that the enemy is just sitting back, watching you walk into your God-given destiny. He'll take his best shots at you. But if you persevere in faith, he will lose.

I'm like a pit bull when I've got a goal in front of me to accomplish. The attacks on me were so severe that many times I thought of quitting. Many times, I thought of how much easier my life was before all of this.

But I encourage you to remember that the further you get into your journey, the more victories that God leads you through, the more spiritual muscle you build. The day will come when you will be grateful that you did not give up and that you did not quit. It is so worth it!

Shawn has to have tremendous faith in God to be used by Him in a manner that can easily be judged on the surface.

There are so many variables to prophetic words that I'd caution you to be very careful of your judgment of them.

I guess the last point I'd like to make is why would anyone need or even want to judge others? Really, how would that even be possible? You cannot know another person's heart. That responsibility is far too great for me. I'll leave that where it belongs — in God's hands. I am grateful that I am not called to judge. I'm called to love.

1 Corinthians 16:14 NKJV, *"Let all that you do be done with love."*

CHAPTER TWELVE

The Preacher's Kid

By now it must be apparent that I learned a tremendous amount from researching, interviewing people and writing the story. It wasn't long before I realized that a person cannot write what they do not understand. If this research and understanding of these stories were the only portion of my learning journey it would have been more than enough.

I'm sure Bernie, Jerry, and Pastor Caleb would all vouch for me in the fact that continually throughout this journey I had many "ah-ha" moments. (An "ah-ha" moment to me represents those times that revelation and understanding suddenly present themselves.) I'm quite certain they found this to be entertaining at times.

I remember one such time being so excited and sharing what I discovered with Bernie only to hear Bernie say, "Yeah, I know. We've been living it for 25 years now." Yes, the learning journey has also been quite humbling at times.

In this chapter, I will share with you some of the many "ah-ha" moments that I encountered along the way. The learning journey that God was about to take me on was quite surprising, even to me.

As you are aware, my dad was not only a prophet, he was also a preacher. You are also aware that I was the epitome of what you think of when you hear the term "PK".

My perception had always been that my wounds came from being John Schrock's daughter. That was at play, but what I missed was the fact that John Schrock wasn't just my dad, he was also a preacher. It was the preacher role that he occupied that brought most of the chaos into my life.

My dad was also an incredible businessman. But being John Schrock's daughter never kept me away from business.

The term "PK" is not meant as a compliment when it is spoken. It refers to the fact that oftentimes it's the preacher's kids that behave the worst. I could write an entire book on the dynamics at play that create such behavior.

In order for you to understand the dynamics at play for a PK, you must understand what it is like to be one. This will give you a bit of a glimpse into some of the things that I faced as a PK.

Perhaps PK's unruly behavior starts because they feel abandoned. They feel as if they have no identity of their own and they want to matter and to be heard. Perhaps it is because they feel like everyone else is more important to their parents and, in turn, to God than they are.

There is an unspoken rule that applies to ministry families, at least in my family it was an unspoken rule. Never tell anyone anything that you hear regarding the congregants, anything that happens in your family or anything that you feel. The only way to know who is friend and who is foe is by taking a risk.

For a preacher's kid, it only takes one bad experience to no longer take risks or open themselves up, especially if the person entrusted has less than honorable motives.

This in itself leads to a lifelong inability to trust people. It also creates an incredibly cynical view of other's motives.

It gets even worse for PKs. If they have a problem that involves their parents (particularly the one in ministry) or a family situation, with whom do they discuss the problem?

Very early in life, the child understands that no one wants to be put in that position. This leaves the child feeling very much alone and with a low opinion of their self-worth.

This can also easily leave the child with negative feelings regarding the church itself and towards Christians in general.

In time, as problems arise, the child, through deductive reasoning realizes that they have two options:

1. Conform to what is expected of you and become complacent. Just accept it, fall in line, blend in, don't draw attention to yourself. Make the best of the cards you've been dealt.

2. Create a life for yourself where you are free to tell the truth and free to live your life with truth.

Guess where that life in the second option can be found?

That's right. They find that freedom and acceptance in the world. How sad is it that it wasn't found in the church? I, myself, fell into category number two.

Ironically, it would have been the church and the teachings of the church that developed the belief system of right and wrong that the child had. The child would view their inability to express the truth and to seek counsel from the church (all the same things that are available to the other congregant) as nothing short of hypocritical. Soon the child views themselves as a victim and wants nothing to do with organized religion of any kind or the God that allowed all of this to happen to them. But that's another book and another teaching for another time.

I find it inconceivable that I never had realized what was actually at play, especially because I analyzed absolutely everything about New Life Church. How could I have gone through my entire life never realizing that my greatest wounds came from the fact that I was a "PK"? It should have been obvious to me if for no other reason than the way that I navigated myself at New Life Church. But it certainly wasn't.

I never saw it or recognized it because I refused to ever put myself back into that situation. Subconsciously, I must have been aware of the amount of pain I associated with it and developed an innate response to not allow it to happen again. Instead of facing it, I had just avoided church altogether.

There is no question that I suffered from many wounds because I was a PK. I honestly had no idea how greatly being a PK had affected me. But God knew and He had a plan.

The Instruction Manual

After Shawn's prophecy, as I was gathering the information to write the book on my dad's life, something quite incredible happened. God woke me up one morning at 4am which was always a time that He'd wake me up to talk to me. This particular morning, He gave me the name and the entire outline of another book, *The Preacher's Kid*.

This book was to be my own life story. God gave me instructions for it, while shutting down the book you are now holding in your hand, the one that Shawn prophesied.

I did not understand what was going on, but I knew without a doubt that that was the book God was calling me to write.

I had no idea of the journey that God was about to walk me through. None! I should have, if for no other reason than the title of the book.

People close to me must have thought I was confused or perhaps I was misunderstanding the direction that God had given me. I, myself, was confused as to what God was doing, but I was not confused about the instructions He had given me.

I knew that it was God because writing a book on my own life would be the very last thing I would ever want or choose to do. This book would make me vulnerable and vulnerability was not something that I liked or was good at handling. I had become a master at self-protection. But God asked me to do it, and out of obedience I stopped writing *The Amish Prophet* and focused on writing *The Preacher's Kid*.

When God shuts something down, you know it without a doubt. This book was shut down.

The Process

God, in His brilliance and in knowing me well, gave me the outline for the preacher's kid to be written in a manner which would share my story but naturally it would include my dad's story.

This book would be a calling back of the prodigals, rejects and all of those people that were wounded by religious folks and/or the church. This was a book that I considered myself profoundly qualified to write. I had spent 30 years of my life listening to other peoples' stories regarding the church and religious people. I completely understood their wounds.

God knew that I would be willing to write the book that exposed my pain because I would be helping to set other's free. In the words of Kris Vallotton, the Senior Associate Leader of Bethel Church, it would give my pain a purpose. Never did I realize that God's intent would be to use this book to set me free. But that was indeed what was about to happen.

As I was obedient to what God wanted and proceeded to write the book on the preacher's kid, I first discovered that I could not write what I did not understand and even worse, what I had not forgiven. I spent well over a year on a healing journey that God Himself took me on and took me through as I was writing the preacher's kid. It was extremely painful to have to revisit the past, but, man, it was worth it.

Interestingly enough, the three people that helped walk me through this healing journey were Pastor Caleb and my dad's partners in ministry, Bernie and Jerry. These men all played the role as Spiritual Father's in my life.

God created extraordinary circumstances throughout this journey. If I was making a trip to Ohio, it would just happen to be that Bernie and Jerry, who travel extensively, would be in town. Or La Red would be hosting a conference that would provide me with unprecedented access to interview many of the people involved in the beginning days of La Red. Every trip would provide me with exactly what I needed at the exact right time. It was nothing short of God's own handiwork.

I knew Bernie and Jerry held many of the stories that I needed, but it went much further than just the stories of La Red.

Bernie had a strong presence in my life since I was twelve years old. He is like a brother to me. He was my dad's right hand for as long as I can remember. It ended up being Bernie that truly would be the most instrumental in walking me through the most painful events in my life.

When I returned to California after my first several trips to Ohio, I returned an emotional mess as the wounds were starting to be uncovered. I did not understand what was going on. I even questioned if it was healthy for these wounds to be reopened. That's when Pastor Caleb would step in to help counsel me through it.

What I would come to realize in time was that the healing that I really needed could only come from my being heard, being understood and being defended. I shared things with all of them that I had never shared with anyone in my life. These were deep wounds that I had compartmentalized throughout my life in an effort to survive.

God used many different plans and created many different situations in my life to bring about healing and to set me free from the burdens that I had carried. One such time occurred when I was in Ohio for meetings with Bernie and Jerry.

Early one morning, I came upon a baby bird sitting on my mom's steps. It must have fallen out of its nest. It could not fly and it appeared that its parents were nowhere to be found. I watched it for a moment analyzing the situation and suddenly I realized what that bird must be feeling. Those feelings of abandonment in me suddenly appeared in me. The floodgates opened and I wept. I was literally doubled over in pain.

My brother J.D. heard me crying and immediately came to find out what the problem was. I showed him the bird, as I could barely speak. I was inconsolable. J.D., without thought, instantly took control of the situation.

J.D. first found a box to put the bird in, then he found a dropper to give the baby bird some water. Next he dug up a worm and cut it up and proceeded to try to feed it to the baby bird.

Watching him try to help that little baby bird abandoned by its parents was completely symbolic of what I had longed for as a child. I was completely and utterly undone.

It would not be long before I was no longer focusing on the baby bird or my feelings of abandonment. I became

undone by the kindness of J.D. It was the most beautiful thing
I had ever seen in my life.

He had such profound kindness in him not just for the
baby bird, but also for me. He did all of this to bring comfort
to me.

The situation with the baby bird also opened up the
floodgates to many memories. I realized that throughout my
life God always made sure that I was okay. Perhaps it wouldn't
always be my parents that were there to provide me with safety
and security. God used many different people and many times
He would use my own brothers.

Clean Lenses

There were so many times that I just wanted to stop this
journey. I was completely out of my element. I knew that I
could stop this freight train at any time and get off if I wanted.
At times, I seriously considered doing just that.

Throughout my life, I had prided myself as being strong
and independent. I was a survivor and over-comer, particularly
when the deck was stacked against me. I would rise to the
occasion and I was driven beyond what is normal to win the
battles that I faced. And win them, I did. It was in my blood. I
came by it honestly!

But God asking me to face an area of my life that I had
literally just run away from was completely overwhelming me.

I had become everything that I hated. I was emotional,
vulnerable and incredibly fragile. Even worse, I had absolutely

zero control in any of it. I was completely dependent upon
God. This was unfamiliar territory for me. I had to have faith
in God beyond faith in my own ability and let go of control. I
had to trust God completely.

I was so tender that tears flowed at the drop of a hat.
I viewed all of it as a weakness. What I discovered is that
allowing myself to experience and feel those things was not a
sign of weakness, it was a sign of strength. It took a great deal
of courage for me to face these wounds. Particularly the ones
that I, myself, participated in creating. Ruthless faith would be
required to get to the other side.

If God would have left my side for a minute, I would have
never been able to handle this emotionally on my own. He
was my counselor, He was my deliverer, He brought me peace,
He healed my wounds and He set me free.

God rewrote my own story as I wrote *The Preacher's Kid.*
My wounds had greatly clouded my vision. He was cleaning
my lenses. I had been viewing my life and my dad through
wounded lenses. Had I written this book first, *The Amish
Prophet,* I am quite confident that it would have been a
different book then what you are reading now.

The Attacks

The enemy took his fair share of shots against me during
this time. I had gone from one extreme to the other. Through
the process of healing, I had progressed from strong and
invincible to extremely fragile and vulnerable. As I experienced

healing from my past wounds, I began to feel free. This newfound freedom led to becoming childlike and overflowing with God's love for absolutely everyone.

The enemy was just waiting for an opening. I had always been extremely cautious of who I allowed into my life to now freely allowing them into my life without thought. Just as I had experienced during my PK years, people with less than honorable motives made their way into my life.

I was so filled with God's love that all I could see in anyone was what God saw in them. I saw the gold in them so to speak. I was seeing who God created them to be, not who they were at present. I did not realize that what I was seeing was meant for me to call out in them, not to extend an open invitation into my life. I completely missed that what I was seeing would require a process for them to get there, just as I, myself, had gone through a process.

After opening myself up, I took three hard and painful hits — attacks the enemy intended to take me back down and to keep me wounded. The attacks were all very different from each other and yet they all hit that same place inside of me that I had previously experienced as a PK.

The hits were fierce because they were familiar. These attacks brought back even more memories of the pain that I had experienced as a PK. One of these would have been more than enough for me to deal with, but with three, I was literally experiencing trauma. I recognized it as trauma because I had experienced it after the death of my father. I was dealing with extreme anxiety. My behavior was irrational and fear was overtaking my entire being. Even my hands were shaking.

The "Ah-Ha" Moment

I did everything possible to overcome these hits, including going through a Sozo at Bethel's Transformation Center. Sozo ministry is a unique inner-healing and deliverance ministry aimed to get to the root of things. It did help me to put things into better perspective, however, I still needed a deeper level of spiritual healing.

I was in unfamiliar territory and at a total loss of what to do. My wounds were so great that I felt uncertain that I was hearing properly from God. I no longer trusted that I was discerning His voice over that of my own. It was then that God provided me with my own personal dreamer, my daughter, Nicole. The dreams that God gave Nicole were relevant to every situation in which I found myself. They held the answers that God knew I needed. It was not uncommon for God to give her as many as three dreams in one week specifically in regard to the issues that I was facing. These dreams served to build my confidence as they confirmed what I was sensing in my spirit but was unwilling to trust.

In time, God revealed to me the plans of the enemy and I boldly refused to be a participant in that plan. I diligently guarded my heart. I made sure not to allow unforgiveness and hatred to infiltrate me. But the pain of these hits was real and it was intense, as my very gifting had been attacked.

This is when God literally removed me from my new little

white church. I was incapable of being there both emotionally and spiritually. Even physically, I reacted to being there. I suddenly became incapable of listening to praise and worship music and any online ministry or ministry on television. Suddenly, everything was shut down. Well, almost everything.

For nearly a year, starting in the fall of 2016, the only comfort and peace that I could find would be in God's word, in the Bible itself. God made it quite clear that everything else was completely off limits. This was the season that God Himself wanted no other voices in my head but His and His word.

God led me to a series of DVDs that were available but actually meant for students in Bible College. These DVDs covered the materials students would normally learn over a three-year time period. They were heavily Scripture-based with most commentary based upon the existing culture during specific events.

Every night when going to bed, I would listen to these DVDs. Every single night I'd fall asleep hearing the word of God. If I woke up in the middle of the night, I'd start them over again. Within six months, I had been through the three-year curriculum several times.

Once again, I had no understanding of what was going on at the time. God always takes me through the situation and then He gives me the revelation. I needed my "ah-ha" moment.

As painful as all of this was, I was going to push through this no matter what I faced. I knew God loved me and I knew

He wanted better for me than even I wanted for myself. I trusted Him completely. I knew if I stayed steadfast and strong and followed His lead that He would take me where I needed to go.

To see and get to experience what was on the other side of this pain became my driving force in life. I didn't care how many mistakes I made, I didn't care how humbling this was and I didn't care what people thought of me or what they were saying about me. I had my sights set on God and only on God. He would take care of the rest. Those were not my battles to fight — He would fight them for me.

In time the revelation would, in fact, come. All of those places inside of me that God had healed, needed to be filled or I would be susceptible to even greater attacks and wounds. That is why the attacks that I had just gone through were so incredibly intense and painful.

God was finalizing my healing by filling me with His word. He didn't want anyone else to teach me. He wanted to ensure that it was solely Him and His word that was being written in my heart and filling those gaping holes that my previous wounds had left open.

I also learned that I needed to establish healthy boundaries and to always seek wisdom, discernment and confirmation from God prior to moving forward, very much like the lessons that the La Red team learned in South America.

This season changed everything for me. My go-to when having problems or questions was no longer Jerry, Bernie or Pastor Caleb. Now my go-to was God and the word of God. I was no longer dependent on anyone — only God.

I could still be in relationship with them, I still loved them, but the dependency was completely broken off of me. As you might imagine it was very freeing.

In time, I was once again able to listen to worship music, go to church and follow other ministries. Everything that had been removed was restored as suddenly as it had been shut down.

God pulled me back up, dusted me off and back on the journey we went.

The Story was Rewritten

Next God shut down *The Preacher's Kid* book. He then released me to write *The Amish Prophet*.

As you might imagine, today, with clean lenses, I see things regarding my life from a completely different perspective. I realized the amount of courage that it took for my dad to follow God's lead when he didn't know where God was taking him. I realized the level of faith and trust in God that it required. I realized that he, too, got to the point where all he cared about was getting to the other side to see what was awaiting him. I realized why the words people were speaking against him had no effect on him. Man, did I get it, as I myself had now lived it, too.

All of this being said, considering everything that God has brought me through, does not negate the fact that there is no doubt a reevaluation of priorities that needs to take place for those called to ministry regarding their families. In the end,

yes, God did step in and brought healing and redemption
to my story because that is who He is and how He works.
However, perhaps it would be best if all of those wounds could
have been avoided. If those called to ministry could realize
that first they need to ensure that they have their own houses
in order before helping everyone else fix theirs.

God has given me a lot of revelation on how I, myself,
partnered with lies. Yes, I was a victim, but in every other area
of my life I refused to wear that label. But I had maintained
the victim status regarding the church and regarding
Christians in general.

I had viewed the "grown up" church as the enemy. The
grown-up church had taken away my little white church.
What I failed to realize is that the fruit of the little white
church was so great, that a new church was inevitable. It's the
natural progression of a move of God.

The grown-up church wasn't wrong, it was just different.
It became home to a huge number of people whose lives also
transformed. Maybe the grown-up church wasn't for me, but it
certainly was meeting the needs of those who attended.

All of this revelation was freeing as the stories in my head
were being rewritten.

Today, I understand and realize that my own parents'
upbringing had also been at play in my upbringing.

I had no real grid for the dynamics of Amish life because
my parents had left the Amish right before I was born. In
time, it became apparent that a portion of the way that I was
raised had a lot to do with the fact that my parents were born

and raised Amish.

Remember when I said that Amish children are shown very little affection and that my dad never heard the words "I love you" from his parents? When I stop to think about that, I realize how big of an improvement that my dad made with his own children, based upon what had been modeled for him.

Likewise, I as a parent, certainly got right with my own children the things my dad had failed at. I am quite confident that my children probably have their own list of things that I failed at. Perhaps what matters is that each generation improves upon the previous one. As the saying goes "our ceiling will be their floor" and they will indeed reach new heights.

Another thing that God showed me was what my life might have looked like had my dad been any less than who he was.

It was estimated by Pew Research Center in 2007 anywhere from 35–42% of people leave the religion they were born into and taught as a child. I was unable to find these same type of statistics pertaining to the 1950's. However, I am confident that number would have been significantly less. I also would venture to say that in the Amish community particularly back in those days that percentage would not have exceeded 2%. The ramifications of jumping the fence were too harsh. This in itself showed how committed John was regarding his newfound belief system. This tells you that something far greater had taken place in John.

Not only did he leave the Amish religion, but as he gained additional knowledge and revelation he also left the

Conservative Mennonite religion. Now the percentages decrease even more because he didn't jump just one fence — he jumped two. He did this in one generation.

He was fearless because he found the truth and he was willing to risk it all to live in the freedom of that truth. He was 100% committed to these newfound truths and to the journey that God placed him on. He believed God!

As I have gone through my own journey with God, I can now totally relate to my dad. Had I gone through this journey at a younger age, I would have more than likely made many of the same mistakes. I have had to make a very conscious effort not to leave my own family behind. I can thank my dad for helping me get this right. It was watching his life that taught me what to be aware of in my own.

Because he left the Amish, lost his family, friends and inheritance, he had no option but to be successful in business. He had absolutely no backup plan available to him. His survival in life was under a great deal of pressure from the moment that he left the Amish.

Although I may not have had a "normal" life based upon the understanding and definition of what that meant to me in my formative years, in some ways I had a truly "extraordinary" life. Today, ask me if I had a normal life and I'll tell you, "No, I did not have a normal life, nor do I longer care." My life was far from the norm, but what I did have led me into a lifelong love affair in the business world.

My father exposed me to the business world during his Mini Merchant days and at 17 years of age, he trusted me to move to Omaha, Nebraska, by myself to run one of their offices. Already at 17, I was fearless in the business arena. Why? Because I watched him succeed with only an 8th-grade education beyond what most people with college degrees succeeded.

Watching his life created a belief system in me that I could be anything and do anything that my heart was set on. My only obstacle would be myself. It never even occurred to me that being a woman could pose a hindrance to me in business. Why? Because I was not raised to believe that.

All of those counseling sessions that I had been privy to as a child provided invaluable insight and training into problem solving and conflict resolution — tools that are hugely instrumental for success in the business arena.

As of 2017, I have spent forty years of my life in the business world and I love it. Every one of my closest friends are a result of a business relationship, that in time and through circumstance, turned into a friendship.

When I think of the strong, male-dominant culture my dad was raised in, his allowing and even encouraging his baby girl to fly could truly have been one of most remarkable transformations in his life. A woman running businesses was absolutely unheard of in Amish country back in those days.

Truly, nothing in my life was ever normal and honestly, that hasn't changed. I've learned to love and actually thrive in unconventional environments. I am not intimidated by, nor am I a respecter of persons based upon titles, positions, wealth or lack thereof. I absolutely love challenging the status quo.

To this day, the people that I am drawn to are the rejects, the underdogs, the misfits and the wounded. Perhaps, I should say they are drawn to me. I'm certain that is due to God's handiwork. They are perhaps the most misjudged and misunderstood people group by the church today. All they need is the right environment, just like the kernel of corn. Their lives will transform. These are the same types of people that you would find at the little white church.

You know the saying, "It takes a village to raise a child?" In many ways I was raised by a village. The majority of my life during my childhood was indeed spent at the little white church, surrounded by that exact thing — a village.

Even today, these people are part my family. Time will never change that. Everyone that was part of the little white church has made a lasting impact on my life.

There is no question that my dad didn't get everything right in his life, but the price that he paid for his children, grandchildren and future generations to live in truth and freedom was worth everything that I might have gone through.

He broke through barriers that normally take generations to break. He was a pioneer and he was a forerunner not just in one area of his life, but in every area of his life.

CHAPTER THIRTEEN

The Fruit

Perhaps, when all is said and done, the best judge of a prophetic word can be found in the fruit from that prophetic word.

Prior to Shawn's prophecy, God was already taking my husband on an incredible journey of his own.

Remember that my husband was Jewish. He was raised that he could believe in anything but Jesus. This was ingrained in him throughout his life.

My husband was privy to my amazing journey and everything that God had taken me through. He was no longer able to reason away all of these things as merely coincidences.

My husband was fully aware of the struggles we faced that morning and how we came to be at Bethel that night. As a businessman himself, he had seen enough to understand that something greater than just a battle over business was taking place.

Shawn's word was the final piece of evidence that he needed to fully accept Jesus as the Messiah.

1 Corinthians 1:22 KJV, *"For the Jews require a sign, and the Greeks seek after wisdom."*

At 69 years of age, my husband was baptized at an impromptu baptism at New Life Church on May 25th, 2015 by our Pastor Caleb Klinge and my cousin, Mark.

If my husband becoming a Christian was the only fruit evident from Shawn's prophetic word — that would have been more than enough for me. That was the greatest desire of my heart. It was nothing short of a miracle. Ask anyone that knows us and knows what we have been through and they will validate the miraculous nature of this.

My children have also been profoundly affected by this word as they have had a front row seat to watch God at work in the transformation of their mom's life.

The La Red ministry was re-enforced with direction at the time this word was given. This word re-energized that ministry.

With having to gather information for this book from Bernie and Jerry, they, too, revisited the purity and the beauty from where God had taken them in the La Red ministry. There is nothing more powerful than revisiting the things that God has done for us in the past to build our faith that He will continue to do so for us in the future.

As I shared earlier, the journey that God placed me on by

writing this book has led to my own life story being rewritten and my lenses have been cleaned. I have faced the many lies that the enemy planted in me to keep me down and to keep me wounded. He doesn't get to do that anymore.

Today I am free, I am healed and I am forgiven for having participated in those lies.

This journey, and God allowing me to see the truth in the situations of my life, has led to my ability to love others more easily. Because of the grace that God has so freely extended to me, I find myself being able to do the same for others.

Remember the story that I shared regarding having been awakened by rain, my first supernatural sign from God? I believe God was showing me what I was about to walk into, representative of this season in my life. I believe that was a sign that He was about to pour out His spirit (rain) in every area of my life, and that I was walking into a season where He would bring healing as well as redemption to my life story. The rain He showered me with, created softened grounds for healing, and the healing created fertile grounds that would yield much fruit.

Today, at 57 years of age, I believe that I am the best version of myself that I have ever been.

As I mentioned, this book required much research. I met with many prophets, I interviewed many people in ministry and I gained an incredible amount of knowledge and insight into the Kingdom of God. This research has taken root in my mind and in my spirit. It has become part of who I am, how I operate, how I see the world and how I see God. He is a good Father!

I don't actually feel like I've written a book on my dad's

life. I feel more like I've written a "success in life" manual. As for every story that I have shared, I have gained a much greater perspective regarding who God is and the operating system that He has established, and how my father was utilized within that system. It's truly been a profound journey.

This prophetic word made me feel known and loved by my Creator. For Him to have called me out to receive a word is humbling to say the very least.

I cannot put a number to the amount of people that contacted me whose lives have been touched by this prophetic word.

I have heard many heartwarming stories from people that have lost loved ones as to how this word has brought them much comfort. They too are reminded as is stated in this prophetic word, "It's a celebration day — that their loved ones are also still alive in heaven right now."

CHAPTER FOURTEEN

Reconciliation

I've shared with you the stories of the naysayers and what my dad had to endure and overcome in order to fulfill the calling that God had placed on his life. What I have not yet shared with you is the reconciliation that God brought to those areas prior to my dad's death. God left no stone unturned in bringing redemption to his life story.

Amish — Family

As you know, John was shunned by his family and the entire Amish community. God knew the wounds that John had suffered when leaving the Amish and losing his family and friends in the process.

It would only be several years after John left the Amish that he would lose his mother and several years later his father.

I remember, as a very young child, sitting in the basement

for both funeral services. I remember feeling scared and knowing that there was something going on that I did not understand.

We were not dressed like everyone else, although we were dressed very conservatively. It was apparent to me that we were being widely discussed among the people. I remember not wanting to be there, but my father insisted that we go.

I never heard my father speak badly about his family. If anything, it was very difficult for him to know that he caused them such great pain and yet he would have loved nothing more than for them to have that same freedom that he had found.

Over the years, one by one, the hearts of his brothers and sisters were greatly softened. So did John's tone. The shunning became a thing of the past. In time, John was able to be in relationship with all of his brothers and sisters.

At my dad's funeral, the church was filled with many of my Schrock relatives. This was no small feat for them as many traveled a great distance to attend. If my dad could somehow see down from heaven, I know he would have had a smile on his face. He loved them all dearly.

Conservative Mennonite

As you know John had first been ordained as a minister at Sharon Conservative Mennonite church.

It was there that Harry Stutzman, David D. Stutzman and Andrew D. Stutzman laid hands on John and set him apart for the work of ministry.

It was a divine appointment where men who represented all the values and principles of the Amish and Mennonite culture laid hands on a young Amish boy. Although in time, John was excommunicated from this church, the values and principles of the Amish and Mennonite cultures forever remained with John.

Throughout the years, a mutual friend kept these ministers updated on the many ways that God was using John to reach the nations. These men were proud of the work that John was doing and referred to him as their son.

In 2009, John was not only reinstated in good standing at Sharon Conservative Mennonite Church he was also asked to be the honorary guest speaker at their anniversary service.

John spoke at this event and in turn he invited Pastor David D. Stutzman to speak at Berlin Christian Fellowship, to which he also graciously agreed.

IFCB — International Fellowship of Christian Businessmen

In 2009, both John and Bernie were invited to Tulsa, Oklahoma, to attend the 20th Anniversary celebration of IFCB. This invite came from Don Hale, long-time President of IFCB and friend of John's. John was also invited to be a guest speaker at this event.

To this day, IFCB still follows the same vision that God had given John back in 1989. They also are doing roundtables and use the "Principles of Proverbs" book in their ministry. Don is a faithful follower of the vision.

Family

As you know, our family time together had greatly suffered because of the calling that God had placed on John's life.

But God did not leave this portion of John's story without reconciliation and redemption.

After John had suffered the blow of the market crash on his businesses, he finally agreed to retire completely from all aspects of his businesses. It was then that he knew that he no longer had the physical or emotional stamina required to withstand the kind of hits that he had always overcome in the past.

After his retirement, he spent a great deal of time by my mom's side helping her work in her flower garden. The two of them went everywhere together. He went grocery shopping with her, took her out to dinner and even bought a second home for them in Sarasota, Florida.

During this time, you could also periodically find him watching television. Watching television was something that John never did unless it was the news. As he always stayed aware of the latest happenings in the world. This was primarily to watch for the fulfillment of Biblical prophecy.

But during retirement, it was not uncommon to find him watching old TV shows. One such show was *The Walton's*. My mom told me stories of the many times that John watched the happenings in this family with tears streaming down his face.

Many times, my dad apologized to me for things that happened in the past, always followed by the words, "I just didn't know." He really didn't know what a healthy family life looked like. For me, that was more than enough. I could see the regret in his eyes as he said those words.

I find it very ironic that as I've gone through the journey of writing this book, that I am now the one sitting here with tears streaming down my face, shaking my head and saying, "I just didn't know."

In the last five years of John's life, we had so much fun together as a family. We all loved to play games and finally he participated in playing them with us. No doubt he was still very competitive and wanted to win when playing them. But just the fact that he was playing them was a miracle in itself.

Every one of us kids that needed to reconcile with him in one way or another were able to do so during these years.

He was a softer, kinder and gentler version of his previous self. It was amazing to get to see him actually play the role of a traditional father to us as well as an amazing husband and companion to my mom. She too had made many sacrifices in her life because of the calling on his.

My dad adored my mom and rightfully so. She was the peacemaker in our family, the glue that held us all together.

As you know my mom's last name is Erb. My dad used to tell people that he heard that (h)erbs are good for you, so he married one.

There was never a question in any of us children's minds regarding how much our dad loved her. He was very affectionate towards her — very complimentary of her, which was certainly unusual back in those days for a man that was born and raised Amish.

My parents had a beautiful marriage and they were very much in love throughout their marriage. All of us kids had a great example of what success in marriage looks like.

Berlin

Berlin, Ohio, which represented a war zone for me as a child could not be more different today then back in those days. Over the years, as tourism entered the scene, many new people moved into the area. This brought about diversity which brought about change.

Although this community still operates strongly based upon religious beliefs, its people have become more tolerant of beliefs other than their own.

In my youth (the 1960's), Berlin/Holmes County was heavily divided based upon the church/religion that you belonged too. This divide dictated not only your friendships but also where you worked.

Today, things have changed so significantly that it is no longer uncommon to find different religious beliefs and denominations within any given family.

This community still operates strongly with good Christian values and principles. You will find some of the most generous people in the country in this community. People will rise up to help anyone in need. They do not just throw money at situations, although they generously help those in need. They truly lend a helping hand.

Today, I have many friends from many different religious denominations represented there. Today, no thought is given regarding the religious group you belong to. The only real criteria you are judged upon is based upon your character. Your word and your actions are everything.

There will never again be any other place that I call home — based upon my definition of home — other than Berlin. Over the years I have grown to love California. However, Berlin holds my heart. I know it always will.

Summation

In the end, it turned out that all of that fighting over religious beliefs and the interpretation of scripture would be nothing short of a waste of time, energy and emotions.

How sad that all of those years were wasted, not to mention the collateral damage endured by those targeted, including me.

Perhaps John's life could serve as a reminder to us all that in the end, God will always set the record straight.

John was not perfect in the way he handled things — no one represented in these stories was perfect. But fortunately, we serve a perfect God, a just God, and a gracious God.

Perhaps we could learn to not jump to conclusions or judgments just because what someone else is called to do may look and be different then what we are called to do.

All of this takes me back to what happened the day after I received the prophetic word from Shawn.

Perhaps this was God's handiwork giving me a bit of a glimpse into what I would be discovering on this journey as I wrote the book.

My husband and I were in our car leaving the prophetic conference to grab a quick lunch. As we were making our way out of the parking lot, a couple flagged us down to stop.

As we rolled our window down to hear what they had to say, we assumed it would be more of the same that we'd been hearing from everyone else. Instead, we were in for quite a surprise.

The man introduced himself and his wife and said they currently reside in Arizona. He proceeded to tell us that his wife was from Berlin, Ohio. He told me her maiden name and asked me if I remembered her or her family. I responded "no," although I did know of the house they lived in.

This man went on to say that unbeknownst to each other, the previous night God had dealt with each of them individually. In the morning, they shared with each other what God had told them the previous night. Come to discover God gave them each the same message — as He was confirming the message to each of them.

God told them that they were to find me and to apologize to me and my family on behalf of the entire Amish and Mennonite communities for the way that we had been treated. WOW! I never believed I would hear those words spoken from anyone. Are you kidding me? Only God!

What a huge waste of time and energy it is to be spending the little time we have here on earth judging, fighting amongst and attacking each other.

I've come to the realization that what may be right for me may not be right for you — and I'm okay with that. That doesn't make me right and you wrong — it simply makes us different. God uses many different people and avenues to reach everyone.

I pray that this book serves as a reminder that we should not focus on our differences. Instead we should focus on what it is that we have in common. This keeps us in relationship with each other.

When I think of my dad's life the one thing that sticks out to me the most is that he lived his life focusing on what he was for — not on what he was against. When you focus on what you are against, all you see are the problems. But when you focus on what you are for — all you see are opportunities.

John's favorite verse from the Bible:
Isaiah 1:18 KJV "Come now, and let us reason together," saith the LORD."

CHAPTER FIFTEEN

The Amish Prophet

By now you must be wondering why I haven't addressed the "prophet" part of my dad's story.

As I told you earlier, I met with many prophets. As I was interviewing people for the book, I discovered several of them were, in fact, prophets. Others literally just presented themselves along the way.

Whether or not you agree that prophets still exist today is not up for debate. For me, it is impossible to deny that they still exist today after everything I've experienced.

The word spoken over my dad at his death, regarding him being a prophet, led me to what I refer to as a treasure hunt. This portion of the journey was by far the most fascinating and the most fun.

I honestly had believed that I was the only person in our family that did not know that my dad was a prophet. I assumed it was common knowledge. I believed that I didn't know because I had been removed from the church scene for so many years. To my surprise it was not common knowledge. No one else in my family knew it either. Although, just like me, it was not surprising to any of them either. We just never thought of him in that particular way. Looking back, it is apparent to me that we should have seen it.

Remember those DVDs that I listened to over and over again? I believe that those teachings contained the answer as to why dad had never told us that he was a prophet. It was in these DVDs that I first discovered this Bible scripture.

Mark 6:4 NIV, *"Jesus said to them, "A prophet is not without honor except in his own town, among his relatives and in his own home."*

And there it was — the answer I had been seeking for years. I know my dad well enough to know that he had read that scripture as a warning.

There was no reason for him to announce it to the world. He knew that God would go before him. He knew that God would speak into the hearts of the people that He sent into his life. He knew that God would equip him with what he needed to help him accomplish what he was being called to do. No announcement was necessary.

I'm also sure he realized that if he had made this known, it would have created a lot of additional problems that were not necessary. I can only imagine the battles he may have faced had this been made known throughout the community. God help us all!

Everyone that knew him knew without a doubt that he walked with major God-given authority.

When I asked Bernie and Jerry about this, whether they knew that dad was a prophet, they both replied, "Yes." It appears that in the circles that John operated in, it was quite common knowledge amongst other ministry leaders. But it wasn't in his home.

Bernie told me that on several occasions he candidly spoke to John, confronting the issue of him being a prophet. He said that John's response was always the same. In the typical John Schrock fashion, he would reply with the words, "As you say."

From left to right: Jim, Joy, Jo Ann, and J.D.

ABOUT THE AUTHOR

Joy Zipper was born and raised in Berlin, Ohio, home to one of the largest Amish communities in the world.

She has spent the last 20 years in the natural and organic food industry, passionately fighting to help improve our food supply, ultimately believing it is a fight to protect future generations. Her heart and soul currently lie with Berlin Natural Bakery where her motto has been, "We do what's right even when it isn't easy." Joy's husband, children and nephew all work together in some capacity in this same industry and each of them is solidly committed to the mission. Joy is also in partnership with a variety of other ventures and has served as a business consultant in a number of industries.

Joy can easily be considered a mother and mentor to many — through both business and divine appointments — and she gives selflessly to every person that enters her life with a need.

She currently resides in Penngrove, California with her husband and love of her life, Alan Zipper.

Visit "The Prophet's Daughter" Facebook page for pictures, fun stories and/or to connect with the author.

For more information about the Amish visit
www.AmishLeben.com.

This website is owned and hosted by my brother, J.D. Schrock. Here you'll find resources and articles to give you a more accurate look into Amish life as well as listings of hotels, restaurants, shopping, and things to do in the area. You can also follow AmishLeben on Facebook.

Additional reading —
Books written by Jo Ann Schrock-Hershberger

Challenges, Choices & Changes
Change Begins With Me
Dynamic Living

Made in the USA
Middletown, DE
19 March 2018